THE MODE

OF

MAN'S IMMORTALITY:

Or, The When, Where, and How,

OF THE

FUTURE LIFE.

BY REV. T. A. GOODWIN, A.M.,

Author of the "The Perfect Man," and late Editor of "The Indiana Christian Advocate."

"With what body do they come?"—*Corinthian Doubter.*
"Thou sowest not that body that shall be."—*Paul's Answer.*

NEW YORK:
J. B. FORD & COMPANY.
1874.

I0835936

Entered according to Act of Congress, in the year 1874, by
T. A. GOODWIN,
in the Office of the Librarian of Congress, Washington, D. C.

DEDICATION.

TO THE LOVED ONES OF LIFE WHO ARE WITH THE LORD

THIS BOOK IS AFFECTIONATELY DEDICATED,

WITH THE CONFIDENT ASSURANCE THAT, THOUGH UNSEEN, THEY ARE EVER PRESENT, LOVING AND BELOVED NO LESS BECAUSE THEY HAVE PUT ON IMMORTALITY.

"Men will linger less in the Graveyard if convinced that the dead are elsewhere."—*Dr. Townsend.*

"Some things that we have read and heard about raising to Immortality the body, the breaking up of graves, and the upsetting of tombstones at the material 'resurrection,' may be questioned without heresy."—*Dr. Daniel Curry.*

"Some believe that these bodies shall rise again. Thank God, not I!"—*Rev. Henry Ward Beecher.*

"We shall be like HIM, for we shall see him as he IS."—*St. John.*

NOTICE TO THE SECOND EDITION.

THE call for a second edition furnishes an opportunity to the author to add a few pages by way of enlarging upon some points, but chiefly in furnishing references to acknowledged scholars and teachers who agree with him on those most severely criticised in the first edition. This is due to a large class of readers who are not averse to the doctrines taught, but who want first to know that they are agreeable to those whom they are willing to follow, before avowing their assent.

The most caustic criticism which the first edition elicited was from an intelligent class of laymen who had heard of late so little about the resurrection of the physical body that they supposed the doctrine had been given up by the better class of divines. Their criticism was that the book was not called for. Singularly enough, at the very time that that edition was passing through the press the *Methodist Quarterly Review* for October 1873 was also passing through the press with an elaborate article from an eminent writer of New England to prove that "*the flesh shall be raised;*" and numerous criticisms elicited from the religious press of the country show that there are yet persons of respectable rank who still cling to that notion. So far, therefore, as that doctrine is mischievous and this work may remove the error from the Christian Church, the book is timely and will be useful.

Not the least of the commendations which the first edition elicited have been numerous testimonials from those in various walks of life who had been led to look upon death and the grave with horror. The more cheerful, hopeful, trustful, Scriptural views herein taught have mitigated the grief they had endured in the loss of loved ones, and removed from their own anticipations all dread of the cheerless charnel-house. The writer is quite content to let those criticise who delight in it, while such results as these follow the reading of the book by the millions who have no favorite creed to maintain, but who wish to drink of the pure waters of the river of life as they flow from the Word of God. That thousands will be made better and happier by reading these pages we firmly believe. None can possibly be made less useful or less happy.

PREFACE.

THIS little book will fall into the hands of some persons who will not read it. A glance at the title-page, and a discovery that the author is not of their rank, will be sufficient. Being great men themselves, they learn nothing from common men. Besides, having made up their minds on the subject discussed, what use?

Others, glancing hastily through it, and discovering that it does not interpret the Bible just as they do, will lay it down with very profound contempt, and probably denounce it as infidel. This is by far the cheapest way to dispose of it. It is the common resort of imbeciles and bigots.

The writer once encountered a representative of this class in the person of a class-leader who had emigrated from the sand-hills of North Carolina. The shape and motions of the earth had been mentioned somehow in a sermon. Deeply grieved and piously indignant, he rushed to the Bible to overthrow the doctrine. "The earth is not round," said he, with an air of triumph. "See here! 'I saw four angels standing on the four corners of the earth.' How can anything be round which has four corners? And the earth does not swing upon nothing. See here! 'Thou, Lord, in the beginning hast laid the foundation of the earth.' How can anything swing upon nothing when it has foundations? Besides that, did not Joshua command the sun to stand still? How could it stop if it had not been going?"

We could not answer him, for he was ensconced behind the Bible, and no argument could convince him that any other interpretation than that which he gave could possibly be put upon those passages, without destroying the authority of the Bible entirely. He died a firm believer that he was right as to the shape and motions of the earth, and that we had grievously departed from the faith as it had been delivered to the saints.

We have met his kith in every walk of life. Our pulpits, and even the professorial chairs of our colleges, have not wholly escaped the tribe. To interpret the Bible in its most literal sense, and to adhere to the interpretation which their fathers gave, is the test of orthodoxy with them. Sand-hillers, whether laymen or clergy, whether presiding at the plow or in the university, need not read this book. They will not like it if they do.

With this inkling as to the style of the book, some will read it only that they may find fault. They will be highly gratified, for they will find something on almost every page to assail. The book asks no quarter. It simply says, in a consciousness of its correctness: "Strike, but hear me."

Some will read it without endorsing or condemning in advance, but, like the good Bereans, will search the Scriptures and exercise good common sense to see whether these things are so. We commend their spirit and judgment. If they are not the happiest class, they deserve to be, for they certainly are the wisest.

The book is written under the conviction that no sentiment is more detrimental to the development of our holy Christianity than that narrow-mindedness which requires its votaries to accept as final the opinions of the fathers as to the teachings of the Bible, or to regard the incidental opinions of the apostles themselves on matters of science, and social relations, and human governments, and physical laws, as above question because inspired.

It was no more possible for the men who were educated in the selfish doctrines of Judaism, modified by the scholarly paganism which surrounded them, to comprehend the scope of the religion taught by the Son of Mary, than it was for our Pilgrim fathers to comprehend religious liberty, or our revolutionary fathers to comprehend the equal rights of man; although their respective formulas embraced the abstract truth.

Seeing that even the apostles modified their views daily on the incidentals of their mission, both as to the scope and intent of the Gospel, why should any Christian teacher insist that the perfection of wisdom and loyalty is found in adhering to the human dogmas of other days?

Will any one say that the Christianity of to-day is not of a higher and purer type than that which obtained when heretics were silenced by the Inquisition; or when witches were burned under its sanction even in our own land; or when sectarian bigotry turned the pulpit into a platform of polemic strife; or when the highest motive to a life of purity was the dread of the lake of literal fire and brimstone? The Christianity of the ages to come will no doubt as far outshine the Christianity of to-day as our type excels that of a century or five centuries ago. The world has outgrown paganism and every false religion because the elements of life were not with them, while Christianity, true to its divine origin, keeps abreast, or rather leads the most advanced phase of human progress.

The apostles and martyrs and confessors never conceived of the far-reaching influence of the words they preached in their healthful influences upon the moral, intellectual, and material interests of mankind. It is probable that the most sanguine Christian of to-day is equally unable to comprehend the higher and purer influences of the Christianity of the ages to come, when, purified and uplifted by the agencies now moulding society, there will be more than poetry in calling the earth, as it then will be, "the new earth," for the former things will all have passed away; but such results will never be attained if Christians are compelled to adhere to the notions of other ages simply because good men entertained them.

This little book goes forth with no pretentions to

great research. It goes, nevertheless, without apology; expecting no favor from a certain class of critics, and asking none. What is true and valuable in it will survive all criticisms; what is valueless will soon be winnowed out and disappear. Its aim is to do good, to create a higher and better standard of faith in the Bible and in the unseen. It will awaken some thought, provoke some discussion, strengthen the faith of some, and possibly do more good than some books much more elaborate on the same subject.

CONTENTS.

THE

Mode of Man's Immortality.

CHAPTER I.

PRELIMINARY OBSERVATIONS—HOW THE BIBLE SHOULD BE INTERPRETED.

THE most noble impulses of our nature lead us to inquire into the mode of that future life which is implied in an affirmative answer to the plaintive question of Job: "If a man die, shall he live again?" There have been so many sunderings of earthly ties—so many whom we have known and loved on earth, and whom we yet love with unabated fervor, have passed into the dim beyond—not to speak of our own personal prospective interests in the question, that he must be lost to the finer sensibilities of human nature who does not often inquire concerning the when, where and how of his immortality. The question loses none of its interest because it is involved in mystery. Even though we may hope to acquire only an approximate notion of the reality, it is yet a study of great interest and importance. In vain do we turn to science or even to revelation for a full and satisfactory solution of this question. It may be that in some sense the Spirit reveals to those who fear God some idea of the future life, yet its realities are not visible to the eye nor audible to the ear, nor can the heart of man conceive of them.

When Paul had enjoyed a special vision or revelation, he apologized for not communicating the knowledge thus derived by saying that it was not lawful for him to utter it, meaning, no doubt, that there was no opening to the human understanding through which such knowledge could enter.* We may be enraptured with the beauties of the rainbow, or charmed with sweet music, yet we do not discourse of music to the deaf nor of colors to the blind, for we say it is impossible to make them understand; because there is no law of nature by which such knowledge can be conveyed to those who have no sense of seeing or hearing. No more can earthly language convey to us a knowledge of heavenly things.

It does not follow because our views may be very inadequate that we, therefore, know nothing and should be content to know nothing about the future life. To know that we shall live again is glorious; to aspire after even an approximate knowledge of the mode of that future life, and to seek a preparation for it, is the most noble aspiration of man.

Whence came the idea of a future existence we can not tell. It has been almost universal in all ages. It may have been transmitted traditionally from the first pair, but more likely it originated from the instinct of our nature which shrinks

---

* Not possible.—*Marginal Reading.*

"Men having no terms of speech fit to express such sublime ideas as the apostle was there taught to understand."—*Joseph Benson.*

"The things which he saw and heard in paradise could not be expressed in human language."—*MacKnight.*

from death and annihilation. To men of our times the conjectures and theories of the most learned heathens of ancient times seem very crude and unsatisfactory. We know, even aside from the light which revelation has thrown upon the subject, that many, if not all, of their notions were false. We know that there is no river Styx under ground, over which the disembodied ghosts of the departed are ferried by a ghostly Charon. We know that there is no Avernus, a gate-way to Elysium or Tartarus, which their mythology had located under or within the earth.

The progress of science, to say nothing of the clearer light of revelation, has long since shown such notions to be absurd and untenable. They were, nevertheless, entertained by educated and civilized peoples—peoples, who, in some of the arts and sciences of civilized life, have never been surpassed. May it not be that the wiser generations of the future will regard some of our notions as equally absurd and untenable? There is nothing in analogy, or in the stability of our knowledge on any such subjects, which certainly forbids such a possibility; for our knowledge on this subject is unlike the truths of geometry, which have been transmitted unchanged for ages. We teach our children, as confidently as our fathers taught us, that the square of the hypothenuse of a right-angled triangle is equal to the sum of the squares of the other two sides; but who can educe from any known truths in science or religion any such incontrovertible proposition relating to the future life that he may insist upon enforcing his views upon others at the expense of social ostracism in case of unbelief?

Is it not strange that, notwithstanding our discarding of the mythology of the ancients, we retain, tenaciously, so many of their views of human immortality? In the conception of most Christians even, to die is to pass over some chilly river. We call it Jordan, they called it Styx; we locate it in the air, they located it under ground. The heaven of the average Christian is the slightest possible improvement on the Elysium of the ancients. It is, like their Elysium, beyond some swelling flood, and when reached, it is a lovely land, abounding with rocks and hills and brooks and vales, and amply supplied with good things for the gratification of the appetite—nothing more nor less than the creature of heathen imaginations, a perpetuation of Elysium, though called Heaven by Christians.

Heaven is, no doubt, something vastly better than all this. It becomes us, with all the light we can command, to inquire concerning it, not discarding any notion because it is ancient, nor blindly adopting any opinion because held by our fathers. The Book of God, that revelation of his will which we call the Bible, is our chief source of information on this subject, as on all others which relate to the origin, character, and destiny of man. It is to be accepted as containing the clearest views of the future life that have ever been expressed, and such is our reverence for its authority that we assume that it as nearly makes us acquainted with the sublime realities of the life to come as can be made known with human language and illustrations, which are designed to reveal the unknown by things known.

But in interpreting and applying its teachings on this subject we are not to accept as infallible the opinions of men, however uniform these opinions may have been for ages. We do not so interpret its teachings on any other subject, but modify our interpretations and accommodate them to every new light, retaining all the while profound respect for the authority of inspiration. Why should the almost unanimous opinions of Christians on the mode of man's immortality, running back even until they are lost in the mythology of the ancients, be accepted any more than upon the mode of his origin and the creation of the heavens and the earth, and the motion and shape of the stars and suns around us?

The Bible is the Book of God. Its essential truths are eternal; but, being communicated in detached scraps of history covering thousands of years, and in poetry of the peculiar oriental style of former generations, containing rapt prophetic visions and referring to habits, and manners, and opinions long since obsolete, it is to be interpreted by a knowledge of the times in which each part was written, and the questionable words of its phraseology are to be understood in the light of modern science and discovery.*

That unwritten Book of God, his works, is no less authoritative than the written Word. Shal-

---

* "It is generally written in the language of common life. Its human authors filled almost every position in life from the humblest to the most exalted. The peculiarities of the writers, their cultivation or the lack of it, the times in which they lived, the dialect they used, the station they filled, are all disclosed in the various books. . . . They had no special knowledge above their fellows as to general science and history. They did not pronounce their revelation in scientific form. . . . The language was human, and uttered in a style to be understood by the half-enlightened people for whose benefit it was first declared. . . . The different authors expressed in their own language, and by their own illustrations, the ideas poured into their minds from on high. . . . The medium was imperfect, and exposes its human limitations and weaknesses. . . . It is not, like the Ten Commandments, a specimen of divine composition."—B. K. PEIRCE, D.D., *Word of God Opened, pp.* 19, 21.

low minds have sometimes thought the two disagreed, and bitter have been the denunciations and persecutions which have attempted to compel an acceptance of man's interpretation as the Word itself; but men of mind have on one point after another conceded that the Word is true, though the former interpretation was false. It will forever remain true that "in the beginning God created the heavens and the earth," although science has demonstrated beyond a reasonable doubt that that beginning may date back millions of years. It is still true that the sun rises and sets, although science long since demonstrated that it is stationary and that only the earth moves.

So in regard to the mode of man's immortality. While no Copernicus has discovered and communicated facts which demonstrate the exact mode of the future life, science has cast at least a doubt upon the commonly received opinions of past ages on some phases of the subject. Can the deductions of science be harmonized with the Book of God, or, rather, can such an interpretation be placed upon that book as shall be consistent with the deductions of science, so far as these are applicable to the subject? Let us see. We speak as unto wise men, judge ye what we say.

We pause just a moment here to say that we are not unapprised of a method of criticism which we must encounter in this discussion. We announce that in this discussion we shall assume, and we hope to prove, that the Bible nowhere teaches the doctrine of a resurrection of the material body, but labors everywhere to teach otherwise, and that science and reason, so far as they can be made applicable to the subject, utterly oppose such a theory.

This will be deemed by many who regard themselves reasonable men as utterly insufferable. We are admonished of this by the style of criticism usually adopted in such a case. Only a short time ago, an obscure but respectable author put forth a book upon this subject, taking substantially the view above announced. It fell into the hands of a reviewer who speaks of it in the following imperious style: "When a writer claims that his individual comment on the Word is the Word itself, in contradistinction to the nearly unanimous exposition of the great body of acknowledged standards, he shows an arrogance that nearly forfeits a right to our attention. Especially insufferable is this when the doctrine, like the bodily resurrection, is one to which all Christendom, whether Greek, Roman, or Protestant, has given its unanimous assent in the most pronounced terms."—*Methodist Quarterly*, 1872. p. 668.

This was received by a certain class of minds as conclusively answering the book by one stroke of the pen editorial, whereas the argument, if such it may be called, is identical in spirit, and almost in words, with that used by the Inquisition in 1633 against Galileo, and by which the Copernican theory of the sidereal movements was *not* overthrown. That imperious body, claiming to be set for the defense of the faith as it had been delivered unto the saints, pronounced the deductions of science as they related to astronomy, "irreconcilable with the letter of the Scripture; . . . absurd, false in philosophy and contrary to the holy Scriptures." Galileo, having by his "arrogance" forfeited all claims to the respect of the Inquisition, was cast into prison until he should recant; but the world moved notwithstanding;

and that Inquisition passed to a future of shame and everlasting contempt, while the imprisoned Galileo lives in honor. The Inquisition had the argument of antiquity on its side. The church, Greek, Roman, and Protestant, had given its "unanimous assent" for ages to the former opinions of the earth's shape and position. Which is the more arrogant, putting forth reasons for a new interpretation, or attempting to silence investigation by invoking antiquity, or civil or ecclesiastic ostracism?

Another preliminary remark: Receiving the Bible with the most profound reverence, as a revelation from God concerning himself and conveying his will concerning us, written by holy men who wrote as they were moved by the Holy Ghost, we nevertheless believe that it contains statements and opinions which are not essential to the central idea, but which, partaking of the traditions and popular notions of the times, answered as scaffoldings for the truth, though not true themselves. The Bible is not to be received as a revised code, with every irrelevant word and phrase eliminated, and the remote truths nicely adjusted. It stands as it was written by kings and by captives, by shepherds and by mechanics, on the throne and in the prison; now history, now poetry, now cursing, now praising, often stating the most important truths and seldom arguing any point; every portion partaking of the spirit of the age in which it was written—ages separated by thousands of years. To eliminate these irrelevant portions and to see God in his real character is the object of Biblical research and study. To allow the Bible student to set aside as surplusage, or as indicating the human instrumentality through which divine truth was transmitted, such phrases as were the mere poetic adornments of the times, or such statements as included the legends and opinions of the times in which they were written—though these statements may be in the form of historic facts, while not facts at all—gives authority to the truth; while to assume that the spirit of inspiration dictated not only the truth, but the evident human imperfections which are mixed with it, drives thousands into unconditional unbelief, who would gladly cling to that which is true and important.

To illustrate: It is not difficult to believe that the Son of God lifted the chronic paralytic from his bed at the pool of Bethesda, and sent him away happy and whole; but when required to believe also that curative properties were imparted to the waters of that pool by the periodic visits of an angel, so powerful and peculiar that any manner of disease could be cured by bathing in the water thus medicated, and that only one patient could go at a time—for there was virtue enough for only one, and he the strongest and most active of all—this staggers the faith of thinking men, and thousands, thus repelled, have turned away from the truth, and have rejected the whole story as an unfounded fabrication, becoming sooner or later unbelievers in Bible teachings altogether.

We can understand how the writer came to record as a fact this legend of the times. There was a great multitude of impotent people at the pool, and they were brought there because of their belief that at times the waters received medical properties through the agency of an angel. It was not necessary for the purposes of inspiration that the writer should make known that this national belief, which had grown in him with his growth from childhood, was an unfounded legend, hence it is introduced as a fact, though only a legend.

Claiming that such a story must be true because the writer was inspired, and that if this be not true no confidence can be placed in any portion of the Bible, weakens the respect which all men should cherish for the history of the wonderful life of the Son of God, and which most men devoutly desire to cherish.

We remark, in passing, that if such passages may not be eliminated from the sacred truths contained in the Bible, as interpolations or unfounded legends, then the Bible is a doomed book, and all its precious truths, with the undying hopes they inspire, are soon to be lost to the world; and it is cowardly and offensive for any intelligent man to say that if such liberties are taken with the Bible its authority as a revelation is lost. Intelligent men accept the Bible intelligently, not blindly.*

Take another example. Nothing is more distinctly stated as a fact than that the waters of

---

* "This *legend* is here neither endorsed nor denied, but merely given to account for the invalid's presence."—*Strong's Harmony, page* 66.

"The evangelist does not seem to do anything more than state the popular *legend* as he found it."—*McClintock and Strong's Encyclopedia, page* 777.

"The verse which speaks of the angel troubling the water is wanting in the most ancient manuscripts."—*De Pressensé, Life of Christ, page* 265.

"The pool was an intermittent fountain."—*Beecher's Life of Christ.*

"I prefer, with the best English writers, to omit the whole passage."—*Dr. Schaff.*

"According to the Jewish popular conception there was a personal angel which produced the moving of the waters. John found this conception, and admitted it to his narrative."—*Lange's Notes.*

"The best Biblical scholars decide that this verse was not written by John."—*Whedon's Notes.*

the deluge covered "all the high hills that were under the whole heaven." For ages this was accepted by "all Christendom, Greek, Roman and Protestant," as stating a literal fact, and questioners of its truth were handed over to the ranks of infidelity without ceremony, for to deny it was to deny inspiration; and it was claimed that without that faith in the inspiration of the Bible which would receive all statements of fact as fact, the Bible could no longer be a book of authority.

But how is it now among men of learning and piety? We know of no modern scholar of respectability who claims any such interpretation for it. McClintock and Strong, whose fidelity to inspiration has never been questioned, say: "We are compelled to adopt the opinion that the flood of Noah was a local event, confined to one part of the earth's surface" (vol. 2, p. 739). This language is specially significant. "We are *compelled!*" It was after a lengthy and exhaustive discussion of the scientific objections to the "uniform opinion" of darker ages. If science, that modifier of creeds, that ruthless encroacher upon old notions, can *compel* the abandonment of old opinions on such a statement of physical fact, why should it be counted "insufferable" to call in question the old interpretations of the Scriptures which relate to the mode of man's immortality?

Again: Matthew writes as a historic fact that some prophet had written that Christ should be called a Nazarene, whereas not a word of that kind can be found in the writings of any of the prophets which have come down to us. Volumes have been written to reconcile the statement with the fact, but there it stands, unreconciled and unreconcilable, yet easily explained by assuming that Matthew quoted from memory a tradition which was current among his people. Such explanations of these discrepancies commend the truthfulness of the record a thousandfold more than the ingenious and improbable conjectures which will be found in the theological speculations of the dark ages.

What is true as to statements of fact is not less true as to opinions. The disciples were entrusted with but one work. Their commission was to preach the Gospel to every creature. What this implied they had not the remotest idea until after the revelations of the day of Pentecost. Only one thought, up to that time, seemed to occupy their minds. Their hopes of temporal power throngh a restoration of the nationality of their people, and the occupying of the throne of David by the wonderful personage whom they had called Master until his unexpected and ignominious death, were revived by the several appearances of the Saviour after his resurrection, but nothing more. There was nothing in his exposition of the Scriptnres concerning himself—nothing in his declaration that such a death was necessary that redemption and the remission of sins might be preached; nothing in his final commission, "Go into all the world and preach my gospel to every creature," which lifted them above their notions and hopes ot the temporal advantages which were to be inaugurated by the Messiah. At the very last moment of the very last interview which they ever had with the Saviour, we find them inquiring solicitously concerning this temporal kingdom: "Wilt thou, *at this time*, restore the kingdom of Israel?"

It required the induement of that spiritual baptism to open their minds to a comprehension of the spiritual character of the mission of Jesus. Now, and perhaps almost unconsciously, certainly unpremeditatedly, they begin to preach redemption and the forgiveness of sins. Peter's first sermon is a model of simplicity, and he was no doubt as much surprised at its effects upon those who heard on the day of Pentecost as he was afterwards when he saw the house of Cornelius converted under the rehearsal of the same simple story of Christ crucified. Henceforth there is a wonderful sameness in the theme of their discourses and the method of handling it: "Redemption through his blood and the forgiveness of sins." On this one subject—the only one committed to them—their views are uniform and consistent to the end, and we accept those views as embracing the mind of the Spirit upon the method of man's redemption. This is certainly God's method of saving the sinner.

But, because we accept their views of redemption so confidingly, and without a question, must we therefore assume that all which they believed, or taught, or wrote, is above question? They had views of social life and views of political rights which were the outgrowth of the times in which they lived; and their national hopes and loves could not be obliterated by such a spiritual baptism as they had received. It is not strange, therefore, that there should occur occasional out-croppings of these in their discourses and letters. The thoughtful Bible student eliminates these opinions as local or transitory, without losing faith in the central idea which they were inspired to understand and to communicate to others—the doctrine of salvation by faith in the name of Christ. The moral and spiritual *doctrines* of the Bible are uniform, and to our faith unquestionably true, while the incidental *opinions* of even inspired men may be as untrustworthy as their statements of philosophy or of science.

Thus, when Paul urges obedience to the powers that be, and denounces resistance to them in such terrible accents, we may admit the wisdom of such sentiments as applicable to those to whom they were written, but we deny *in toto* their applicability to our revolutionary fathers, or to any others who resist tyranny and oppression. If Paul spoke by authority in the second verse of the thirteenth chapter of Romans, every one of our revolutionary fathers has long since suffered the pains of perdition.

It is mere trifling to say that he meant that it was a damnable sin to resist a good government, for he says nothing about good or bad government, but he was in fact writing in behalf of as bad a government as ever existed—one which, only a few years later, lighted the streets of Rome with the burning bodies of Christians. This is a human opinion, interjected into Paul's greatest epistle, of merely local and prudential application, and it is the business of Scriptural exegesis to eliminate such from the important and general teachings of the Word of God.

Again, who but an incorrigible fossil believes that the authority of inspiration attaches to what Paul wrote about the silence and subjection of women? Received in its most obvious meaning, it forbids their preaching and praying in public so unmistakably that some of the largest and most educated denominations of Christians have not yet recovered from the prejudices and absurdities transmitted from the Papal church;

and they yet so religiously adhere to the authority of Scripture, as they allege, that they will not tolerate the public preaching or praying of women. And they are right, if all of Paul's *opinions* are equally binding upon Christians. By the exercise of good common sense, by comparing Scripture with Scripture, and by making allowance for the age in which this was written, and the people to whom it was written, and the occasion for which it was written, other Christians find no such an inhibition. In this way all Scripture should be interpreted and applied.

If, then, in these items of opinion Paul was speaking only from his national prejudice and narrow views of the scope of Christianity, may it not be that other opinions held by him, outside of the specialty of his life, were equally erroneous? In this discussion we shall assume that at one period of his life he did entertain such erroneous notions. To what extent and for what intent we may take this liberty will appear hereafter. If the reader is not willing to allow this, he need read no farther.

One more preliminary remark: If in the discussion of this subject we shall appeal to the Bible as authority and yet reject some of its most positive teachings as the literal construction of the words would imply, we must not be counted a sinner above all others, nor as impeaching our own witness upon which we rely for light upon the subject under discussion. There are many passages of Scripture which will not bear a literal interpretation. It should not be counted strange if some of these be found relating to so obscure a subject as the mode of man's immortality, and it can be no answer to our argument that, in some instances, we do not accept the grammatical construction of the words, if we keep within the general teachings of inspiration and of reason on the subject under discussion.

To illustrate: David says, "The wicked go astray as soon as they are born, speaking lies." Whatever that means, it is not literally true. Again, Jeremiah says: "They have sown wheat but shall reap thorns." That was a physical impossibility in Jeremiah's days, just as it is now. "This *is* my body, this *is* my blood," never was true, and never can be. Wine is not blood, and the Papist who teaches transubstantiation from this text, whose authenticity has never been questioned, only insists upon the same method of interpretation that some of like spirit would force upon the reader of the Bible on other texts. Does any sane man insist upon a literal acceptance of this passage: "Except ye eat the flesh of the Son of Man and drink his blood ye have no life in you"? Yet it is in connection with this doctrine, so repugnant to our senses, that the promise to raise man up at the last day is found, which is a chief, if not the most direct and positive proof of a resurrection of the material body.

If we cannot accept the first clause of John vi., 54, in its literal sense, why must we believe the latter: "Whoso eateth my flesh and drinketh my blood hath eternal life, and I will raise him up at the last day"? Both are at war alike with experience and human reason. Again, it is written: "Every one that believeth on the Son, I will raise him up at the last day." (John vi., 40.) This is a proof-text of a general resurrection of the material bodies of men, yet only a few verses from this we have: "He that believeth on me, out of his belly shall flow rivers of living water." (John vii., 38.) Shall we accept this in its literal sense, too? It predicates upon faith in the Son, a physical absurdity and impossibility not one whit greater than that of a restoration to immortal life of the dust which once composed the bodies of men. We know the former is not literally true, why should we insist on the latter? To oppose scientific objections to a bodily resurrection is no worse than to oppose the same to this latter text.

Dare any Christian to interpret literally the language of Christ: "I came not to send peace upon earth, but a sword"? Yet not one text can be found in the whole Bible half so pointedly declaring the doctrine of a general resurrection of dead bodies at the end of the world.

The injunction to wash one another's feet was received in its literal sense by the early church. The Church of England carried out the letter of the command in early times, and there are not wanting sects to-day who insist upon it as a religious rite. "Greet one another with a holy kiss" is as much an inspired injunction as is Paul's anathema against the sin of rebellion, and as much inspired as some of his opinions relating to the end of the world; yet why should those who do not kiss each other on meeting charge us with a want of reverence for the Bible in eliminating such passages as evidently refer only to times and customs and opinions long since exploded?

Taken in its literal sense, the Bible is not only a compilation of most absurd injunctions, but it contains numerous contradictions. "I and my Father are one" is a direct contradiction of the text: "My Father is greater than I." "No man hath seen God at any time" is wholly irreconcilable with: "He that hath seen me hath seen the Father."

There is a rational and satisfactory method of disposing of these textual inconsistencies, which not only relieves them of their offensiveness, but brings them into harmony with each other and with other Scriptures, and makes them tributary to the great truths intended to be taught by God's Word. It is a puerile question which is sometimes asked with an air of wonderful concern: "If I may not believe this or that passage in the most literal sense, then what may I believe?" We answer, we cannot tell what *you* can believe. *We* believe the whole Bible, as interpreted by reason and common sense, and by the Bible itself. If, because *you* cannot believe, for instance, John vii., 38, in its most obvious meaning, therefore *you* cannot believe anything,—you are much to be pitied. You are, however, in the large company of infidels which dogmatism has made for ages.

The learned Bradford K. Peirce writes: "The literal meaning is to be given to all words unless it will cause them to express what is inconsistent with universal experience as to the nature of things, or with the declared opinion of the sacred writers in other passages. When the literal meaning asserts that which is known to be impossible, it must be given up." Paul writes: "The letter killeth, but the spirit giveth life."

CHAPTER II.

THE BIBLE TRUE, THOUGH MIXED WITH HUMAN ERRORS. THE BIBLE-ACCOUNT OF THE ORIGIN OF MAN. THE SPIRIT IS THE MAN.

WE have indicated in the foregoing chapter the spirit in which we appeal to the Sacred Scriptures for light upon the mode of man's immortality. In our heart of heart we cherish a most profound reverence for the things revealed, which are able to make those wise unto salvation who receive the truth in the love of it; and we shall not be driven from our confiding trust in the Word, as thousands have been, by that narrow bigotry which more than insinuates that unless we accept this Word as wholly unalloyed by traces of human imperfections we cannot receive it at all. Gold is none the less gold because it is often found imbedded in flinty quartz, or mixed promiscuously in the sands under foot. To separate it from the one or the other is often a work which requires both patience and skill; and, because of this, many an adventurer has prospected only superficially, and retired disgusted and disappointed, bearing false reports of the mines; just as many a superficial reader of the Bible has denounced it as a jumble of meaningless contradictions, because he would not exercise the patience and research which are required to *look into* this "perfect law of liberty." This has been one fruitful source of infidelity.

On the other hand, the most virulent type of infidelity has found its origin and chief nurture in that narrow-mindedness which requires from all an acceptance of everything found in the Bible as equally inspired, and of equal authority, and all to be construed and accepted according to some formula of the creeds or not to be accepted at all. More than once this style of enforcing the truth has well nigh driven from the Christian standard the cultivated men of the age, as it did in the earlier stages of astronomical and geological discoveries and deductions; for astronomy and geology were at first tabooed as infidel.

It was the absurd dogmas of the Roman Church which made Gibbon and Hume and such men the unbelievers they were. Later dogmas of Protestantism, in one form or another, have in like manner driven from the communion of the church many valuable men, because, with little less persistence than Rome herself, we have insisted upon our interpretation of the Bible being accepted as the only safe passport to heaven. As our good Pilgrim Fathers fled from England to avoid persecution, yet became the most intolerant of persecutors, so, many narrow-minded bigots are found in the ranks of Protestantism who lack only the power to become first-class inquisitors.

The happy mean lies between these two extremes. There are golden nuggets of truth in God's word to be had for the searching; and we should encourage every man to examine carefully the things that are written, before denouncing them as untrue; while, on the other hand, we should extend the most cordial greetings to those who may not be able to deduce from the mine of truth just the same formula of faith that we receive, while the heart trusts in our Saviour, and the life is regulated by the precepts of the Bible.

In the discussion of this subject from a Bible stand-point, we call attention first to the remarkable uniformity with which the Scriptures speak of the spirit or soul as being the man himself. There are, indeed, many references to the soul and to the body as only a part of the man, in deference to the prevailing opinions of the times and as a convenient form of speech; but in no case, except in Matthew's account of one of Christ's discourses (x., 18) are soul and body coupled together as constituting man, while in Luke's account of the same discourse this phrase is omitted (Luke xii., 5); thus at least neutralizing whatever argument might be adduced from Matthew, proving the duality of man.

But if the complete nature of man can be proven by this process, we set Paul against Matthew, and prove that he is triune, and composed of spirit, soul and body (1 Thess., v., 23), and we set Mark and Luke against both Paul and Matthew, and prove that he is composed of "heart, understanding, soul and strength" (Mark xii., 33), or "heart, soul, mind and strength" (Mark xii., 30; Luke x., 27), each of which leaves the body out of the composition, altogether—unless the word "strength" may be taken as referring to it.

It furnishes a rational solution to these seeming discrepancies to say, in the language of Dr. B. K. Peirce: "The Scriptural writers did not pronounce their revelation in scientific form" (*Word of God opened*, p. 20). Paul wrote to the Thessalonians using the Greek philosophy of man, while Matthew used the Roman anthropology, neither pretending to teach the exact nature of man.

The most usual language concerning man speaks of soul and body, spirit and body, outer-man and inner-man, or, in modern language, matter and mind. To this division we shall confine ourself as being both rational and Scriptural, leaving it to those whose tastes seek nicer distinctions to build him of as many parts as they choose; two, three, four, or five, for they have equal Scripture for all.

We repeat that there is great significance in the oft-recurrence of such language of inspiration as attributes to the soul or spirit, or the immortal part, all the qualities of a complete personality, the *ego*, the *I myself*, of our existence. To our mind the account of creation, as given by Moses, finds its most rational interpretation in a recognition of this truth: that man exists, independent of the body, an entire and complete man. We will not speak dogmatically, but we ask the same method of interpretation which the acknowledged facts of astronomy have forced upon the other statements of this record. It is no greater a departure from the opinions of the fathers than that which is now uniformly allowed among educated men as to the creation of the earth, and the sun, and the stars. The assertion may be assailed as a new departure, and no demonstrations of physical science may suggest or corroborate it as in the departures which astronomy and geology compelled, yet we suggest it as beautifully harmonizing with the other doctrines of the Bible, especially those which relate to the mode of man's immortality; and as relieving a seeming contradiction of the inspired historians.

The record of man's creation is as explicit as it is short and beautiful. It reads thus: "And God said, "Let us make man in our image after our likeness: and let them have dominion over the fish of the sea and over the fowl of the air, and over the cattle and over all the earth, and over every creeping thing that creepeth upon the earth; so God created man in His own image, in the image of God created He him, male and female created He them."

This is a complete history of the creation of man. It includes not only the fact but the motive and the manner of his creation. He is created in the image of God, that he may have dominion over a part of the works of God. "A little lower than the angels, crowned with glory and set over the works of His hand" was David's notion of his relative rank and dignity. He was, when created, according to Moses, "in the image of God:" he shall be, in his immortality, according to Christ, "as the angels of God."

This image and likeness represented God, not as the photograph represents the person. It was not merely a picture of God, but it represented God *as Christ himself represented the Father*.

Paul calls man "the image and glory of God," and he says of Christ that he is "the image of God," "the express image of His person," "the image of the invisible God." Hence, in whatever sense Christ represented the Father, being like him, in that sense and no less does Paul teach that man was made in the image and likeness of God, unless good reason can be shown why one image of God differs from another image of the same being, or why Paul uses identical language to represent essentially different things.

That phase of infidelity which professes to accept the Bible as of divine authority, yet emasculates it by omissions and interpolations to suit theories of possibilities, has tampered with even this essential truth, and sought to make the word conform to its notion, by interpolating in the text such phrases as: "in righteousness and true holiness," "in moral nature," "in moral character." It is like the work of the same infidelity upon the beautiful and significant prayer of the apostle: "That you may be filled with all the fullness of God." It does not quadrate with the infidel theories of God and of man that all the fullness of God may be imparted to man, hence there is injected into this significant expression the word "communicable," to make God's word conform to infidel notions of possibilities, and make it read: "that ye may be filled with all the *communicable* fullness of God." Give us rather the truth as it is written, and let us have it in its divine fullness, whether we can comprehend it or not.

"In the image of God created He him" is the unchangeable truth. One drop of water is not the ocean, yet it is like the ocean in every respect but its magnitude. Man is not God, but he is like God in every respect but His infinitude. God is a Spirit. The creed says: "without body or parts;" but the Bible, which ranks the creed, says nothing of the kind. It speaks of God's face, and hands, and heart, and feet, and eyes, and ears. But that pious infidelity which dares not reject the Bible, yet will not believe it because with our bodily senses and earthly experiences we can not comprehend how there can be a hand that is not material, or a foot that is not physical, or an eye whose lenses are not like ours, gravely and impiously explains away the truth which it cannot comprehend, and teaches that God has no body because He is not material, and no parts because He is a Spirit, and yet, forsooth, they discourse occasionally of a spiritual body which they expect to wear by and by. With them this spiritual body is conceivable, because, in their theory, the matter which composes their limbs and eyes will be used in some way to make a spiritual body of, while God, not having had an anterior material existence, can have no body or parts, having had no body to be changed from matter to spirit.

The history of man's creation might have closed with the 27th verse of the first chapter of Genesis, and have been complete. It does close there, and is complete. When Moses wrote: "In the beginning God created the Heaven and the Earth," he closed one complete chapter or epoch of creation. When he wrote: "And God said let there be light, and there was light," he closed another complete chapter or epoch of creation. So, also, when he wrote: "So God created man in His own image; in the image of God created He him, male and female created He them," he closed another complete chapter or epoch of creation.

How far back that beginning was, the mind of man cannot conceive. We talk of millions of ages, but we know nothing of what is implied by such a phrase. The child looks upward and sees a blue vault which it calls the sky, but there is no vault, no sky there. It is only the limit of the human vision. Thus we may go backward in our thoughts, yet beyond the line which terminates our conceptions the beginning was, and God was still beyond that.

Geology is not yet, and probably never will be, an exact science, but its teachings are so uniform and conclusive that no man of average intelligence any longer disputes so much of its teachings as fixes the beginning alluded to by Moses in the very remote ages, measured by millions of years; albeit there were men less than half a century ago, in high ecclesiastical position, who answered the doctrine much in the spirit, and almost identically in the language, of the inquisition of the seventeenth century. It was contrary to the uniform opinions of the church in all ages and repugnant to the word of God.

It is as deducible from the text that the present order of things followed immediately upon the event recorded in the first verse of the first chapter of Genesis—that the sun, moon and stars were not made until the fourth day, and were then hung around that immense body which we call the earth, as servants and ornaments to this great centre of all creation, as that the subsequent history of man followed instantly upon that which is recorded in the 27th verse. For anything which may be deduced by analogy or learned from the record to the contrary, illimitable ages may have intervened also between the creation of man and the beginning of the history of our race as given by Moses. The statement of his creation, like that of the creation of the earth, and the light, and the stars, is concise, comprehensive and complete. While we do not insist that it need date one hour, or one second, anterior to the embodiment of man, there is every reason, from the record and from analogy, to believe that through all these ages man existed in the likeness of God, a spirit, as the angels of God, and discharged the special duties for which he was created.

Geological research has unearthed no fossil remains of the pre-Adamic man, for he was not material in his nature. He had no "form" made of clay to perish or to be preserved, but it does not follow, therefore, that he did not exist. There were fishes in the sea, and fowls in the air, and cattle in the field, through all those ages of preparation; why may not the man who was created to have dominion over them have lived also? It will certainly not be claimed by any modern scholar that beasts, and birds, and fishes, and vegetation, were for the first time created at the beginning of the Adamic period, although for untold ages, and, indeed, until within a half century, that was the "unanimous opinion" of all who received the Bible account as authentic.

The earth had teemed with animal life long before the time of Adam, and death had done its work upon the successive generations which had been, while vegetation had flourished as it never has flourished since.

In the fullness of time, after the numberless geological changes which deposited gold here, and coal there, and granite yonder, by processes which we but imperfectly understand, the Infinite chose to make a form for man of the gross material which belongs to earth, and thus for a season to ally him to the earth as he never had been allied before. The account of this transaction is found in the 7th verse of the second chapter, and reads thus: "And the Lord God formed man of the dust of the ground, and breathed into his nostrils the breath of life, and he became a living soul," not a compound of soul and body, as the heathen supposed, and as some Christians who derive their notions more from the classics than from the Bible yet believe. Everywhere in the Bible this "form," this earthy body, is spoken of and treated as being something outside and distinct from the man. Paul calls it the earthly house of this tabernacle—a mere temporary abode for the man which inhabits it. The phrase, "And the Lord God formed man of the dust of the ground," can mean nothing but that he made a form for man of earthy matter.

It may not be amiss to notice that the Hebrew verb which is rendered *formed*, in the 7th verse relating to man and in the 19th verse relating to the lower animals, never occurs in the Bible in the sense of create, or to make out of nothing, which is the primary and almost exclusive meaning of the verbs used in the 26th and 27th verses of the first chapter, and in the first and second verses of the fifth chapter. Its usual meaning throughout the Bible is to *fashion*, or to *frame*, or to *form* something out of that which had a prior existence. Thus, Psalms xciv., 9: "He that *formed* the eye"; xciv., 20: "That *frameth* mischief"; Isaiah xliv., 9: "*Make* a graven image"; Isaiah xliv., 12: "*Fashioneth* it with a hammer." It sometimes has a widely different meaning, as in Isaiah xi., 13: "Judah shall not *vex* Ephraim," and in Psalm xx., 28: "Mercy and truth *preserve* the king;" and in Isaiah xlix., 8: "I have *helped* thee." A very significant use of the substantive form of the word is found in Psalm ciii., 14: "For he knoweth our *frame*, he remembereth that we are dust," alluding to the fact of *framing* man of dust—making a frame for man, as we might well say.

But, at best, such a philological argument is unsatisfactory, and it is introduced here merely as cumulative or corroborative, not as conclusive or material. The best method of reaching the meaning of such obscure passages is to compare them with that Scripture whose meaning is well known and obvious. To our mind it is plain that the meaning is that he made a form, a frame, a body, for man, of the dust of the earth; in other words, he clothed man with an earthy body, or an earthy garment, or an earthy *frame*.

We must bear in mind that in every account given of the *creation* of man, it is always stated that he was *created* in the likeness of God. This statement, found in the first chapter, is signally emphasized in the fifth. "In the day that God *created* man, in the likeness of God *made* he him." Nothing like this is found when referring to the *forming* of man, the making of a form or frame for man. This *forming* or framing was identical in nature with the *forming* of the beasts of the field, *out of the ground*, as noted in 19th verse, and all chemical and philosophical tests demonstrate that the flesh and bones of man are identical in every constituent element with its kindred flesh and bones, that of animals, made like his "out of the ground." Of each it may be said, "dust thou art, and to dust returnest."

Turning to other Scriptures we find a beautiful and conclusive exposition of this account of the forming of man. Paul speaks in 2 Cor. iv., 1, 4, of the body as an earthly house, a tabernacle which may be dissolved without destroying, or in any way affecting, his personal identity, but only enabling the real man to enter at once into the heavenly house. He maintains the same idea, Phil. i., 22: "If I live in the flesh," and again in the 24th verse: "To abide in the flesh," while he calls dying a departure of himself from this fleshly abode to be with Christ. He means the same thing in Gal. ii., 20: "The life which I now live *in the flesh.*" The *man*, Paul, lives *in the flesh*, and he expects to live out of it when he departs from it.

The same doctrine is unmistakably taught by Peter. He says (2 Peter xiv.): "As long as *I* am in this tabernacle." The ego, the man himself, lived in a tabernacle, a temporary tent, nothing more. He then speaks of death as "putting off *my* tabernacle"—something which belongs to *me*, but not any part of *me*. He puts it off as a man puts off a garment. Again, like Paul, he calls the present life, "living in the flesh" (1 Peter iv., 2) living in a tabernacle of flesh. This habitual style of speech cannot be accidental or without significance.

There can be no mistaking the meaning of Paul when he says: "I knew a man caught up," but whether in body or out of the body, he could not tell. With him the man was still a man, though out of the body. He says nothing of the ghost or spirit of the man, as constituting only a part of the man, but speaks of the man himself.

Much less significant, yet not wholly irrelevant is the language of Job: "Thou hast *clothed* me with skin and flesh and *fenced* me with bones and sinews." (Job x., 11.)

If, therefore, Paul and Peter were correct in regarding the body as a mere tabernacle, which would only be "put off" at death, a house in which they lived, and from which they would "depart" when done with it; if Job was correct in regarding his body as his clothing, the conclusion is irresistible that the *forming* of man, the *framing* of man, was but the making of this tabernacle, the making of this clothing, the making of this frame, which is of dust, (Ps. ciii., 14,) and that this material organism is no part of the man.

This exposition of the Mosaic account of man's early life will, however, not be accepted by those who have, by any process, come to believe that the after-life will be so unlike the present life that there will be no father or mother in heaven, no son or daughter, no husband or wife, no brother or sister, because it has been revealed that there will be no conjugal relations there. They are almost willing to forego the fond anticipations of such recognition as ninety-nine-hundredths of Christians entertain, rather than to believe that man could have existed in a pre-Adamic state as male and female. Why they might not they cannot tell, except that there can not be sexual distinctions in the spirit life. Let those who entertain so cheerless a view of the life to come entertain it if they can; the millions of believers expect to recognize the loved of life as they knew them here. If they may, then pre-Adamic man in the spirit form of the Father may have existed as God created man, male and female; for, "*in the day* that God *created* man, in the likeness of God *made* He him, male and female *created* He them, and blessed them, and called their name Adam (the man) *in the day when they were created.*" This covers the whole act of creating. They were created in the likeness of God in *the day*—at the time—that they were created. They were *created* in *the same day*, evidently at the same time. But the record of the *forming* of the male man is one thing, and that of building the woman another. The male was formed "out of dust of the ground." Subsequently a garden was planted eastward in Eden, and this man, all alone, was put into it to dress and to keep it. During this period of loneliness he was commanded not to eat of the tree of knowledge. It was also during this unmated state that the work of naming all the cattle, and all the fowl of the air, and every beast of the field was performed. It is an unwarranted assumption to suppose that this was done by any supernatural process. It must have consumed some time, perhaps days, and possibly weeks or years. But however short the time, it was *because* among all the living creatures which were brought before him, there was no companion for him, that woman was made.

The account of this transaction is so connected with the work he had just accomplished that no other construction can be put upon it. The conjunction "but" can have no other work in this sentence than to thus make the building of the woman a sequence of the discovery. "And Adam gave names to all cattle, and to the fowl of the air, and to every beast of the field; *but* for Adam there was not found a help meet for him." It was after this that the deep sleep fell upon him and he lost a rib and found a wife.

As in the account of the forming of the male man—the making of a form for him, so in this a verb is used whose primary significance is to build, and it is rendered "builded" in the margin. It is the verb which is rendered build in Gen. viii., 20; x., 11; xii., 7, 8; 1 Kings vi., 1;

xviii., 32, and often elsewhere. A form was *made* for man of the dust; a body was *builded* for the woman from the rib of the man.

To another class of Bible scholars this exposition will be easily answered by the fact that the command to multiply and replenish the earth occurs before the statement of the forming or embodying of man in his earthly house is recorded. They find no difficulty in the anachronism by supposing that the seventh verse of the second chapter is only a restatement of the same fact in another form as that recorded in the first chapter. But when we desire to use it as relating to a distinct and subsequent event, the anachronism means everything.

This objection cannot be answered to the satisfaction of those who believe that the comprehensive sentences of that first chapter record events just in the order of their occurrence. He who believes that the first creative fiat made only the earth and its heavens, and that other minor works filled up the other intervening three days, or three geological epochs, or three thousand years, until, on the fourth day, God made the sun and moon and millions of fixed stars, which are suns much larger than our sun, and that he then judiciously spread them out around our great earth for its sole use and benefit—he will find in this statement of the command to multiply, in advance of the account of the forming of the body, an unanswerable argument, but nobody else will. As those who believe such an absurdity are very few, and altogether beyond the reach of reason, we shall not try to satisfy them.

The Bible, therefore, teaches nothing more clearly and constantly than that the mind is the man. No other one thought is so uniformly presented as this. Paul means to state a fundamental truth when he says the first man was made a "living soul," not a compound of matter and mind, of soul and body. This idea begins with the first chapter of Genesis, and, permeating the whole book, is repeated in almost the last verse of the last chapter of Revelation. In the first he is presented as a pure, holy spirit, the image and likeness of God; while in the latter he is unalterably filthy or holy, as his moral character had been during the period of his earthly probation. It is not said: "let the *soul* of him that is unjust be unjust still, and the *soul* of him that is filthy be filthy still," but the language is used of the man, and that, too, of the man disembodied, or unclothed. Not even the omnipotence and holiness of God are so frequently and constantly presented as this fundamental truth. The Bible teaches the spiritual character of man or it teaches nothing concerning him.

But the theory of the mode of man's immortality which is contained in this book is not dependent wholly or even chiefly on the correctness of the exposition of the Mosaic account of his creation herein discussed. With unshaken confidence in its correctness, it is introduced merely as corroborative of the general teachings of the Bible, to be alluded to hereafter, and it is no more to be despised than the arguments are which are drawn from the nature of the matter which enters into the body, so much like all other matter that it may well be said to have been made of dust, while the common language of life and the uniform sentiments of all peoples are worthy a place in any argument upon this subject.

We speak of the integrity and entirety of a man, though first one limb, then another, and another, and another is amputated, until there is left only the casement of the vital organs, and even that may survive the limbs for years, and at last become all gangrenous and effete; at every stage, to the very last, he is a man—a whole man, either in law or in the esteem of his acquaintances, though only a loathsome fragment of the physical form remains.

Neither does an occasional mention of the soul, the man, as "my soul," or "my spirit," indicate that the body is a part of the man.

But it is suggested that Paul's prayer, "Your whole soul, body, and spirit be preserved blameless," and "Present your *bodies* a living sacrifice," and "Your bodies are the temples of the Holy Ghost," all indicate that the body is a part of the man, because it is included in the scheme of redemption. We answer that this no more proves such a thing than the injunction under the Old Testament, which is continued under the spirit of entire consecration in the New, which required the bells, and pots, and fields, and flocks of the children of Israel to be sanctified to the Lord, proves that they, too, were the subjects of grace and a part of the man. The idea is the same under each dispensation: all that a good man is or has belongs to God.

If it be insisted as an answer to all this reasoning that the record says he formed *man* of the dust of the ground, using the word *formed* in the sense of *created*, the argument proves entirely too much for its own friends. If the material body which was fashioned or formed out of pre-existing material is the *man*, then that alone is the *man*; for the wildest dualist has never insisted that the soul was made of dust. The record does not say that he formed a part of man of dust, and then completed his manhood by introducing an immortal soul. In whatever sense man was formed of dust, the entire man was formed; hence the body becomes the man, and the breath of life which was breathed into him became no more a part of him than the steam becomes a part of the machinery to which it imparts motion and power, except that by this inspiration the *man*—that material *form* which was made of dust—became a living soul. This is an empalement upon an uncomfortable horn of their own dilemma, and proves that after all man is closely related to other animals; for that dust, that clay, was dust of the ground, and, like all other dust, had been enriched by the decay of the animals which had lived and died in the millions of ages which had preceded the introduction of man—the making of man out of dust which had in all probability once entered into the organisms of the extinct races of former geological periods. Is this the God-like man, made in the image of the Creator?

In concluding this chapter, we wish to say that we have sought to arrive at the true meaning of inspiration in the account of man's creation, by that legitimate process of comparing Scripture with Scripture, and keeping constantly in mind the underlying truth of the whole Bible: that man was *created in the image of God.* As a material being, he could not be thus created; hence we conclude that this record shows that the mind is the man. The spirit, or soul, is the image of the Invisible Father. Dr. Whedon, in his notes on John iv., 14, beautifully expresses the Scriptural idea, "Herein God and incorporeal man agree, that both are mind, personality, or spirit, and being of the same nature, they are able to blend and commune, spirit with spirit." The views of Bishop Butler will be found in a foot note at the end of Chapter XV.

CHAPTER III.

THE MODE OF IMMORTALITY AS TAUGHT BY JOB.

ANY discussion of the mode of man's immortality, which would examine the teachings of the Bible, must of course include a review of what is said in the book of Job; for more frequent allusion is made to the future state in that book than in all the Old Testament beside. When Job lived, or who he was, is not material to our purpose, further than to say that it is probable that he lived at least two hundred years before Abraham, and, therefore, not less than six hundred years before Moses. Without detracting from the authority of his opinions we must notice that they partake of the prevailing notions of early ages and embrace doctrines that we now know to be false.

Misled by the popular fallacies of the times relative to the shape and position of the earth, Job, in common with the nations of antiquity, believed that there was a world under this world to which the dead went; and this the Hebrews called *Sheol*, while the Greeks called it *Hades*. To men of modern thought this seems like a strange delusion; but it is not so strange that the generations believed it who regarded this earth as a horizontal plane of limited dimensions, around which the heavenly bodies made their diurnal revolutions, as that men who know that this astronomical notion has long been exploded, by the discoveries of science, should yet retain not only the language, but the faith of those times of ignorance and superstition, and retain in their theology a *Hades* for the dead, simply because Bible writers, using the language of their times, and being no wiser in the philosophy of things than their neighbors, wrote of such a place as the abode of the departed. When driven by their better knowledge of the physical world from the absurdity, as to the locality of a place for the dead, they cling to the existence of such a place somewhere in the universe of God, because Job and David believed there was a receptacle for the dead; and because Bible writers speak of it (a blunder and absurdity which underlie much of the false philosophy yet in existence concerning the mode of man's immortality); never seeming to think that an enlightenment which removes it from that cavern under the ground takes it forever from the realm of actuality. If there be no *Hades* where Grecian mythology located it; no *Infernus* where Roman philosophy placed it; no *Sheol*, where Hebrew superstition put it, then there is no more a *Hades* than there is a river *Styx*, or a cave *Avernus*, or a river *Lethe*. It is just as legitimate to prove from the Bible that there must be some palace for the sun such as the Greek fables represented when they pictured him coming forth with his winged horses; for the Psalmist says the sun has a tabernacle, and "He cometh out of his chamber and rejoiceth as a strong man to run his race." It is beautiful poetry with David, adopting the notions of his times concerning the whereabouts of the sun during the night, yet that does not make the existence of such a chamber or palace a reality, though David believed it as firmly as he believed in the existence of *Sheol*, and upon the same authority.

Because, in their creed, the relative position of this world of spirits was beneath or under the earth, the common expression was that to die was to go downward—down to *Sheol*. It embraced more than the literal lowering of the body into the grave, and included the supposed descent of the spirit to the dark unknown. Any reference to a return to earth, or to life, would, therefore, be expressed as a coming up, or a rising from the dead, and hence the word resurrection became applicable to the act of returning, and also to the state of those who had returned. The argument so flippantly used by those who believe in the dogma of a future general resurrection, and so conclusive as they suppose, that because the Saviour and the apostles used the word "resurrection" in its popular sense, without explanation, therefore its etymological meaning must indicate a fact that we dare not question, is just as valuable and conclusive as that, because the same authorities used the words rising and setting as applied to the sun, therefore, the sun rises and sets, just as the popular opinion of that day maintained.

The extreme sufferings of Job led him to speak familiarly and frequently of death, but his views were but little if any above the notions of his times, notwithstanding they are often referred to as authority by a certain type of Christian expositors. He says: "As the cloud is consumed and vanisheth away, so he that goeth down to *Sheol* shall come up no more. . . . Let me alone, that I may take comfort a little, before I go whence I shall not return, even to the land of darkness and the shadow of death; a land of darkness, as darkness itself; and of the shadow of death, without any order, and where the light is as darkness. . . . Man dieth, and wasteth away: yea, man giveth up the ghost, and where is he? As the waters fail from the sea and the flood decayeth and drieth up, so man *lieth down* and *riseth not*. Till the heavens be no more, they shall not awake, or be raised out of their sleep."

There is in all this a distinct avowal of a faith in man's immortality, but there is not the remotest allusion to a bodily resurrection. His *Sheol*, the abode of the departed, was not only underground, but it was a land from which there was to be no return. "He shall come up no more;" "I shall not return;" "man riseth not;" "they shall not awake," were the gloomy, cheerless views he entertained of those who enter that land of darkness, that shadow of death. It was, indeed, a land of conscious existence, but no pleasure or joy was anticipated therein.

Some, intent on proving the doctrine of a future bodily resurrection, even at the expense of making Job contradict himself, construe his poetic allusion to the eternity of the heavens as the measure of the duration of man's continuance in that land of darkness, so as to teach that by and by, when the heavens shall be no more, then man shall awake and be raised out of his sleep. Such a perversion of the plain meaning of any man's language for any purpose is reprehensible, but when it is undertaken with the language of Scripture to bolster an untenable dogma of man's invention, it becomes unpardonable. What respect could we entertain for any man who should announce that Watts believed that immortality would ultimately end and that then his days of praise would cease, and attempt to prove it by quoting the following lines from that poet?

> "My days of praise shall ne'er be past,
> While life, and thought, and being last,
> Or Immortality endures."

Such a perversion of the plain intent of the poet would deserve the scorn of all honest men, yet the language is almost identical with that of Job. The perpetuity of one thing is predicated upon the acknowledged eternity of another. The argument is the same with Job and with Watts.

But we are told that in the nineteenth chapter Job declares in favor of a bodily resurrection. That is the very thing that he does not, even remotely or by inference. His language, as given in the common version, is: "I know that my Redeemer liveth, and that he shall stand in the latter day upon the earth and though after my skin, worms destroy this body, yet in my flesh shall I see God, whom I shall see for myself and mine eyes shall behold, and not for another, though my reins be consumed within me." It is noticeable in the first place that the translators, who were believers in the doctrine of a future resurrection, notwithstanding that thereby they make Job contradict his oft-expressed views elsewhere, inject into the text the words, *day*, *worms*, and *body*, which are not in the original. Almost any dogma can be maintained by thus doctoring the Scriptures.

A literal translation of the original would read very nearly as follows: "I know that I have a living kinsman and that at last he shall stand in the field. Although they [diseases] shall not only consume my skin, but the fat and muscles under the skin also, nevertheless, I shall see God in the flesh. With my eyes I shall see him, and not another for me."

If there is anything prophetic at all in this text, it refers to the coming Messiah, his living kinsman, whom he expected to see incarnated.

The passage may be aptly paraphrased thus, if it refers to any far off event: "Let my words be written; let them be engraved with an iron pen and lead in the rock forever, for I know that, bankrupt and diseased as I am, I shall have a kinsman who shall be my Redeemer, I may now be consumed by diseases, yet he shall stand at last in the field of strife, having overcome all foes; and I shall see God clothed in my flesh. I shall see him for myself, and no others shall see him for me."

It is impossible to reconcile Job's gloomy views of the after-life, so often expressed, with the hope of a resurrection, which this passage has been distorted to teach. He was as much inspired when he wrote the fourteenth chapter as when he wrote the nineteenth, yet in that he bemoans the fate of the dead in this most striking comparison: "There is hope of a tree if it is cut down that it will sprout again and that the tender branches thereof will not cease; though the root thereof wax old in the earth and the stock thereof die in the ground, yet through the scent of water it will bud and bring forth boughs like a plant. But man dieth and wasteth away, yea man giveth up the ghost and where is he? Man lieth down and riseth not."

Would he have written in this doleful strain had he entertained a Christian's hope of immortality? Would he have written thus if he had believed that to die was to be separated from the body only a little while and that then soul and body should be re-united all glorious and immortal?

So untenable indeed is the argument heretofore derived from Job that it is almost wholly abandoned by late Biblical scholars, even by those who suppose that elsewhere they find in the Bible the doctrine of a bodily resurrection. While the commentators of the last century and the early part of this were almost uniform in discovering an allusion in these verses to the far-off bodily resurrection, the abandonment of this by the best writers of late years is so general that we should not feel justified in referring to the old interpretation, except that we know it to be commonly received and preached as a proof of a bodily resurrection. The chapter on Job, in McClintock and Strong's Encyclopedia, disposes of the whole subject in this significant sentence: "The later doctrine of the resurrection of the body is not found in this poem." We therefore dismiss Job with the conviction that there is no resurrection of the body taught by him, or even hinted at.

Dr. Townsend, one of the Professors in the Methodist Theological school at Boston, though a believer in a general resurrection of some sort, thus disposes of Job: "The true meaning of this passage is easily discovered if we embrace in our view the whole drift of the afflicted man's argument. He had been repeatedly charged with a want of integrity. His friends and enemies had told him that his sins were the cause of his misfortunes. In his heart he knew that this was false. He had faith that his past course would soon receive vindication, and that his integrity would be proved and acknowledged. The harmony of the entire book of Job depends upon taking this view of the subject. The passage may be paraphrased thus: You suppose that I am forsaken of God on the account of my sins. It is not true. To be sure I have not the means at present to disprove your position or establish mine, but I believe that though I am now suffering and may suffer still more, even until the worms eat my skin and then eat into my body, yet in my flesh, on the earth, and before I die, I shall see and you will see my vindication."

CHAPTER IV.

THE VIEWS OF JACOB, SAMUEL AND DAVID.

PURSUING our inquiry into the teachings of the patriarchs on this subject, we next find Jacob, nearly four hundred years later, giving his opinion. The immediate occasion of his uttering his faith was the calamity which he supposed had befallen Joseph, who had recently gone from him in the flush of young manhood; but whose clothes are before him all torn and bloody, with the information that they had been found in this plight, under circumstances which indicated that Joseph had been devoured by wild beasts. What does Jacob say? Among many other things he expresses his opinion of his own and of his son's immortality thus: "I shall go *down* into the grave *unto* my son." He did not mean the grave, for his son had not been buried, but had been devoured by wild beasts. Even then his flesh and bones were becoming a part of their flesh and bones, but he thinks of his son as living still, not a naked ghost, but the veritable Joseph in the *Sheol* which his times had fitted up, *under or within the earth*, as the place for departed spirits. Jacob did not say that the soul of his boy lived, meaning only a part of the man, and that his own soul, as a part of himself, would rejoin it shortly, and that after awhile the beasts of prey would restore the body of the boy and that the grave would give up his own body. There is not the remotest allusion to any such a faith. He simply says: "I, Jacob, myself, shall go down to Joseph, my boy, and then we shall see each other again."

Years pass in the history of the people which had been chosen as the depositary of truth, before we find another incident from which we can deduce the notions entertained by them concerning the mode of man's immortality. Samuel, the faithful prophet, had died, and God had forsaken Saul. In the madness of his abandonment he sought an interview with Samuel dead, whom he had utterly contemned while living. Accordingly he visited a woman familiar with spirits, or in modern phraseology, a spirit-medium. The language used in the interview is suggestive of the notions of the times. The woman asks: "Whom shall I *bring up* to thee?" And Saul answers: "*Bring me up* Samuel." Here we have, five hundred years later, the same ideas of death, and of the future life. To die was to go down to that under-world called *Sheol:* a notion not altogether abandoned to this day, except that we send the wicked only downward, while we send the righteous upward so as to fix a great gulf between them!

The phraseology is further suggestive. The dead retained their individual personality and identity. There is no calling for the ghost or spirit of Samuel, but for Samuel himself, and the veritable old prophet came, a little displeased, as he well might be, at this disturbing of his quiet for so insignificant a purpose; and he talked with Saul. Among the instructive passages in this account of spirit manifestation is this: Samuel said to Saul, after much other conversation: "To-morrow shalt *thou* and *thy sons* be with *me*." He does not say thy soul or ghost, as a part of thyself, shall be with my soul or ghost, the immortal part of me, but *thou* and *thy sons*, whatever constitutes your personal identities, shall be with me, myself, my veritable person. We may have occasion to allude to this incident hereafter as illustrative of an important law of spirit-life.

Not many years afterwards David was called to part with a child whom he dearly loved. The circumstances were such as to call out his ideas of a future life, and to commit the same to the record. When he perceived that the child was dead he ceased to lament and fast, but went to the house of God and worshiped. In explanation of this unusual conduct he says: "*I* shall go to *him* but he shall not return to *me*." There was no dividing of his child into soul and body, and no allusion to any far off resurrection. To his mind the child continued to live, not indeed in that lovely casket, but in the land of immortals, whither he too was going. It lived, a veritable child, though absent from the body, and he was to go to him, a veritable man and father. The body was no doubt tenderly cared for, and suitably laid away, and so were the little garments which he had worn, and all for the same reason, the association which each had had with the child now gone on before—he had worn both.

Years afterwards, when about to die, he said: "Before *I* go hence, to be no more," still clinging to the idea that his personal self should depart, using substantially the language of Paul and Peter under similar circumstances.

We call to mind no other incident in the Old Testament which developed the sentiments of patriarchs or prophets in regard to the mode of man's immortality, except that in the account of the death of each of the patriarchs it is said, "and he was gathered unto his people," evidently intending to teach a continued personal existence of the real man in another mode of life.

We see how, in most respects, the opinions of these Bible characters correspond with the notions of surrounding nations. In the opinion of each, there was a vast receptacle for the dead somewhere under ground. The heathen poets more elaborately define this place, giving the Cave *Avernus* as the opening to it; and there is no reason to believe that the *Sheol* of the Hebrews was any farther away from the earth than the *Infernus* of the Romans. It was a vast cave within the earth or under it, supposing the earth to be a flat, thin surface. And, as we have already hinted, the demonstrations of science, which reveal that what is under us at this hour will be above us twelve hours hence unless it is within the earth, have not materially modified the opinions of those who choose to accept old notions as true, without troubling themselves to notice their absurdities.

Though there was this similarity in the views of the ancient Hebrews and surrounding heathen nations, and though the future of the best of the patriarchs was cheerless as compared with the hereafter of Christians, yet it was incomparably better than the fabrications of the heathen poets, which have, by the way, contributed so largely to many modern notions of the future life. While these made their *Infernus* a receptacle of ghosts, as only a part of man,—where they should be tormented by furies and harpies, only a very few of them drinking of the waters of oblivion and returning to the upper world, to return again to the shades, after having inhabited another body, and so on endlessly,—the *Sheol* of the Hebrews was a place in which *the man* should dwell, disembodied, it is true, yet in the society of those once loved on earth. There is a world of beauty in David's faith, bordering indeed on that of Paul. He not only expected to meet his departed babe and the lost of life, but he expected to be in the society of his Lord and be like him: "I shall be satisfied when I awake with thy likeness."

CHAPTER V.

Isaiah, Hosea, Ezekiel and Daniel.

WHILE there is nothing in the writings of these prophets which relates to the mode of the future life, if indeed there is any reference to a future life at all, it is proper that we should refer to the few passages which, strangely enough, are supposed by some to prove the doctrine of a future general resurrection.

David is sometimes quoted, (Ps. xvi., 10,) "Thou wilt not leave my soul in *Hades* nor suffer Thine holy one to see corruption." There is no future general resurrection here, even if we were at liberty to wrest it from its specific purpose. We have the best of authority for referring the whole of this Psalm to Christ, in whose resurrection it was fulfilled most literally. His body was raised the third day, having seen no corruption, but that can not be a pattern or example of the resurrection of bodies which have for ages been consumed into dust.

Isaiah has been quoted as though he taught that the dead bodies of men would rise at some future general resurrection: "Thy dead men shall live, together with my dead body shall they arise. Awake and sing, ye that dwell in the dust: for thy dew is as the dew of herbs and the earth shall cast out the dead." (Chap. xxvi., 19.)

It would seem, indeed, that Isaiah did teach a literal resurrection of dead bodies, in spite of

Paul's declaration that flesh and blood can not inherit the kingdom of God, if he had been speaking of a future life at all. But alas for such a conclusion! he was dealing with temporal affairs altogether; and such as were in no enviable condition. He was speaking of the future of his *nation*, not of himself or of the world, speaking of temporal things, not of eternal things. Take the connection and read, beginning at the twelfth verse:

"Lord, thou wilt ordain peace for us. . Other Lords have had dominions over us: but by thee only will *we* make mention of thy name. *They* [other Lords] are dead, *they* shall not live, *they* are deceased, *they* shall not rise, therefore thou hast visited and destroyed *them.* Thou hast increased the *nation*, . . . thou hast removed *it* far unto the ends of the earth. In trouble *they* visited thee, *they* poured out a prayer when thy chastening hand was upon *them.* . . *We* have been in pain, *we* have as it were brought forth wind. *We* have not wrought any deliverance in the earth neither have the *inhabitants of the world* fallen. Thy dead men shall live, my dead bodies shall arise. Awake, and sing, ye that dwell in the dust, for thy dew is as the dew of herbs and *the land of tyrants* shalt thou cause to fall. Come, *my people*, enter thou into thy chambers, hide thyself for a little moment, until the indignation be overpast, for the Lord cometh out of his place to punish *the inhabitants of the earth* for their iniquity."

In this grouping together the text and the context, we have omitted no word or phrase that was necessary to the connection or meaning. We have taken the liberty of giving a literal translation of so much of the nineteenth verse as is depended upon to prove the doctrine of a future general resurrection, and when thus translated there is not the semblance of resurrection left; as the context shows there is not even in the common version. We appeal to every Hebrew scholar for the substantial correctness of this translation.

Whatever may be intended by this graphic description of national humiliation and national deliverance, the resurrection of the bodies of all men at some future time is not in it at all, even as the common version stands. We have yet to find a commentator of respectability who assumes that the doctrine of a future resurrection can be proven by this passage. They uniformly apply it to some deliverance of the children of Israel, but generally follow Bishop Lowth in saying: "The deliverance of the people of God from a state of the lowest depression is explained by images plainly taken from the resurrection of the dead." Indeed! But that is assuming the very thing which needs proof. The Bible nowhere teaches such a resurrection; why should prophets illustrate temporal deliverances by the creature of uninspired imaginations?

Identical in import is the prophecy of Hosea written a few years after the prophecy of Isaiah: "The iniquity of Ephraim is bound up, his sin is hid. The sorrows of a travailing woman shall come upon him. . . . I will ransom *them* from the power of the grave. I will redeem *them* from death. O death, I will be thy plague! O grave, I will be thy destruction. . . . *Samaria* shall become desolate," etc. (Hosea xiii., 12–16.)

Turning to Ezekiel we fare no better. In the thirty-seventh chapter is a remarkable vision which has been tortured times and ways without number to prove or to illustrate the doctrine of a future general resurrection. It would be amusing, if the matter were not so serious, to listen to the thousand eloquent and pathetic discourses which have been "founded" on this vision; all containing graphic descriptions of the rattling among dry bones which Gabriel's trumpet is supposed to cause at that great day.

Only one commentator that we have been able to consult is entitled to any respect in the interpretation of this vision, yet, strange to say, the commentators who deduce resurrection from it almost wholly ignore him. He was, however, rather a good old man, though a slave, and he lived once on the banks of the river Chebar, and his name was Ezekiel. He thus comments: "These bones are the whole house of Israel. Behold they say, our bones are dried and our hope is lost. We are cut off from our parts. Thus saith the Lord God: behold, O my people, I will *open your graves* and cause you to come up *out of your graves*, and bring you into the land of Israel. And ye shall know that I am the Lord when I have *opened your graves*, O my people, and brought you up *out of your graves*, and shall put my spirit in you and ye shall live, and I shall place you in your own land. Chap. xxxvii. 11-14.

This was Ezekiel's interpretation of Ezekiel's vision, yet in the face of this we find Bishop Lowth and his followers saying: "It is also a clear intimation of the resurrection of the dead." The Bible, as a revelation of truth and as a guide to man, loses its authority with thinking men, when those who claim to be its expositors thus pervert it.

The only other passage in the old testament

which is claimed as proving the doctrine of a future general resurrection is that in Daniel, chapter twelfth; "And many of them that sleep in the dust of the earth shall awake, some to everlasting life and some to shame and everlasting contempt. And they that be wise shall shine as the brightness of the firmament and they that turn many to righteousness, as the stars, forever and ever." (Verses 2, 3.)

In the next verse he is commanded to shut up the words and seal the book to the time of the end, which proves, we are told, that this refers to a general resurrection at the end of the world, whereas Daniel never wrote a word on that subject in his life, and never even dreamed of it, so far as his dreams have come down to us.

The time of what end, forsooth! Certainly not the end of the world, if indeed the world is ever to have an end according to the popular notion on that subject. Turn back to verse fortieth in the preceding chapter and let Daniel explain Daniel. It will be seen that "the time of the end" is rather a lively time, after all, according to this commentator. It reads thus: "*At the time of the end* shall the King of the South push him, and the King of the North shall come against him, like a whirlwind; with chariots and with horsemen, and with many ships, and he shall enter into the countries and shall overflow and pass over."

That certainly does not sound much like the scenes which are usually supposed to be connected with the end of the world. Yet this is "the time of the end" to which Daniel was to shut up the words and seal the book.

Reading further, we discover that there was something else doing at this "time of the end" besides awakening from the dust of the earth: "He shall enter into the glorious land and many countries shall be overthrown. . . He shall stretch forth his hands upon all countries and the land of Egypt shall not escape, and he shall have power over the treasures of gold and of silver, and over all the precious things of Egypt. . . . But tidings out of the East and of the North shall trouble him, therefore he shall go forth with great fury. . . . And at that time [the time of the end] shall Michael stand up, . . and there shall be a time of trouble such as there never was since there was a nation, even to that same time [the time of the end,] . . . and many of them that sleep in the dust of the earth shall awake, etc.

There is not a word in all this which can by any acknowledged law of exegesis be construed into even hinting at the resurrection of dead bodies at the end of the world. It is a graphic description of national disturbances, but nothing more. Even if the resurrection of the dead were alluded to, it would be fatal to the common theory, for only "many" shall awake, not all, as the theory of the general resurrection requires.

What is said about the relative honor and shame of the two classes alluded to was fulfilled to the letter, on the return of the children of Israel from captivity. Many who, like Ezra, and Nehemiah, and Habakkuk, had remained true to their religion during the darkest days of the captivity, did shine as the brightness of the firmament, and literally awoke to everlasting life. They live yet in the hearts of all who love true patriotism and a spirit of self-sacrifice for the good of others, while the timid, time-serving crowd, who abandoned all national aspirations and became Chaldeans in heart and life, lived only in shame and contempt in the new Israel which followed the captivity.

These four prophecies refer to the same event in the history of the children of Israel. Isaiah's and Hosea's were written in Judea more than a hundred years before the captivity. These prophecies not only foretold the captivity and the manner of it, but its end and the manner of that also, and the 26th chapter of Isaiah and the 13th of Hosea are parts of that prophecy. Ezekiel's prophecy was written among the captives and during the captivity, more than a hundred years later than Isaiah's and Hosea's. What Isaiah and Hosea had so accurately foretold as to the humiliation and overthrow of that people was a painful reality with Ezekiel, a part of which he was himself; but the marvelous deliverance had not yet taken place. It is fitly described by the vision of dry bones. He uses the same figure concerning the restoration that Isaiah and Hosea had used, at least a hundred and twenty years before—the opening of graves; and he, by the authority of God himself, applies this figure to that event.

Daniel wrote about fifty years later than Ezekiel, yet before the return from the long captivity, and he uses the same illustration, the coming forth of dead men from graves.

Whether either of the subsequent writers knew what those before him had written is immaterial. It is probable he did, yet these are separate and distinct prophecies, extending over nearly two hundred years; and all so minutely fulfilled that no comprehensive work on the fulfillment of prophecies has ever omitted to notice them. They stand out as testimonials in behalf of the spirit of prophecy which is one of the bulwarks of our holy religion. Why should they be wrested from their legitimate use and made to do service in the cause of error?

It is little less than impious to say that, the teaching of the Bible being in favor of a general resurrection, these prophecies may be applied in this way. The preacher of historic renown whose soul was grieved at high head dresses in a former period of their prevalence, and who hurled anathemas at them from the words "top not come down," (Matt. xxiv, 17,) gave as an apology that the spirit of the Bible was against high head dresses, and he was, therefore, justified in distorting this passage to suit his purpose. To apply these prophecies to prove or even countenance the doctrine of a general resurrection is not any better, but it is worse by so much as the subject is one of greater interest and magnitude than the style of a woman's bonnet. His sermon was as legitimately drawn from his text as is the resurrection of the bodies of men inferred from these prophecies.

CHAPTER VI.

Christ's Teachings with the Sadducees, by the Narrative of the Rich Man and Lazarus; by His Conversation with Martha; by the Transfiguration; by His Conversation with the Dying Thief.

HAVING failed to find the doctrine of a general or special bodily resurrection in the Old Testament, let us examine the New Testament for the views of the mode of man's immortality there taught. Let us examine carefully and candidly, for neither the writer nor the reader can have any motive for deceiving or being deceived. The writer would not unsettle the reader's faith if he could, for any less purpose than to make him happier, while the reader should not refuse to carefully examine the truth because of pride of opinion or the dread of innovation. We turn to the New Testament with much assurance, for life and immortality were brought to light—were illustrated—by the Gospel. All that man can know of the future life is taught in this latest revelation of God to man, unless it be those supplemented teachings of yet imperfectly recognized pyschological phenomena which seem to bring the hidden life somewhat within the range of human experience. To learn, therefore, what it teaches is to acquire all attainable knowledge on this subject; hence it should be studied not only by its own light, but by all the light which science and experience can throw upon it.

At the time of the coming of Christ, the Jewish people did not believe in human immortality as generally as in the earlier and purer ages of the nation. During the dark period of their history which intervened between the closing of prophetic vision and the dawning of the Day Star, a period of about four hundred years, they had substituted the vilest traditions for the pure doctrines of their fathers; making divine service to consist of mere form, utterly ignoring the spirit of worship, and materializing everything. Prayer was no longer the communion of a humble heart with the Divine Father, but it had become a form of vain repetitions, or a species of self-laudation, with bitter denunciations and contempt for others. The Pharisees, who were the extreme literalists of that day, were prompt to tithe the meanest of garden herbs, but they cared nothing for justice or mercy. There was not a requirement of the decalogue which they had not abrogated by their materialism. Tradition had become supreme, and legends were held in greater esteem than the authentic facts of their national history.

The doctrine of man's immortality had not escaped this general demoralization. Living among an educated heathen people, and being in political subjection to them, the Jews were more likely to descend to their level than to lift the heathen to the plane which the Hebrew people had occupied in the days of David and Solomon. Among other defections they had substituted the heathen notion of the compound nature of man for the sublimer Scriptural idea of the divine image being the man; and they spoke of man as being composed of soul and body. They had adopted the heathen idea of Tartarus, but had transferred it from the regions below to the dismal valley of the Sons of Hinnom, near Jerusalem; and retaining the idea of burning as the punishment of the wicked, Gehenna became the hell of their times, and a place of perpetual burnings. Those who did not wholly ignore the doctrines of immortality which their fathers held fixed up a bungling compromise between the teachings of inspiration and the doctrines of the heathen, and believed that at some future time the body would come forth from the grave and be reanimated by the soul, and that soul and body would dwell together for ever, the good in some place above the earth, the wicked in the burning flames of Gehenna, near Jerusalem.

It is not strange, therefore, that a large and influential sect, called Sadducees, arose and, contemplating the absurdity of the popular notion, swung to the other extreme and denied the doctrine of immortality altogether. Similar materialistic doctrines at a later day have contributed to a like result. But the Sadducees were false in their conclusions, because they were false in their premises, as we shall see.

No doubt they had often confounded, if not convinced, the Pharisees by presenting the logical results of their doctrine of the resurrection of the bodies of men; and now they approach Christ with the confusion which must result from such a resurrection as they had been taught to expect. "In the resurrection whose wife shall she be?" they asked, with an assurance that if the seven men all claimed the one woman there must be trouble. The answer is conclusive as against the Sadducees, and is valuable for all time, as throwing more light upon the mode of man's immortality than any other lesson in the Bible. "Ye do err, not knowing the Scriptures nor the power of God." There is in this at once a rebuke and an apology. Ye do err, but your error grows out of a misapprehension of the Scriptures on the subject of man's immortality, and in not understanding the power of God. The mode of the future life is not what ye have been led to believe. It is not gross and material, but purely spiritual; "as the angels of God in heaven," therefore, "they neither marry nor are given in marriage;" and he might have added, no doubt, if the question had embraced it, that they neither eat nor drink, nor sleep, nor die.

It will be seen by the thoughtful reader that this answer is leveled quite as much against the false doctrine of the Pharisees as against the false conclusions which the Sadducees drew from it, although the immediate intent was to refute the conclusion that there is no resurrection—that is, no future life.*

---

*That the Greek word, *Anastasis*, in every case in which the context does not otherwise fix its meaning, refers to a future existence, without any reference to a coming up of the body, is the testimony of learned men of all ages who have had the candor to express their opinion. How it came to be so used is clear from the prevailing notions of ancient times, that to die was to go downwards —for the soul to go *down* to the *Hades* of early times. To live again or to continue to live would naturally be expressed by some word which implied a return. The Greek verb from which this noun is derived simply means to *stand up* or to *stand again*, a position which implies life. Dr. Dwight, a man of unquestioned learning and fairness, thus comments on this word:

"This word is commonly but often erroneously rendered 'resurrection.' So far as I have observed, it usually denotes our existence beyond the grave. Its original meaning is to *stand up*, to *stand again*. As standing is the appropriate position of life, consciousness and activity, and lying down the appropriate posture of the dead, the unconscious, the inactive, this word is not unnaturally employed to denote the future state of spirits who are living, conscious, active beings. Many passages of Scripture would be rendered more intelligible, and the thoughts contained in them more just and impressive, had this word been translated agreeably to its real meaning. This observation will be sufficiently illustrated by a recurrence to that remarkable passage which contains the dispute between our Saviour and the Sadducees. 'Then came to him the

We shall refer hereafter to the puerile evasion of the force of this answer, as against a bodily resurrection, which assumes that the Great Teacher here meant to say that in the resurrection—in the future life—so much of the body as constitutes the sexual distinctions will be omitted, because they will not be needed where there are no marriages. The occasion was one too important to justify such trifling. In rebuking their materialism he excepted all of the body to which their question referred, and by just inference he thus excepted the whole body.

The doctrine of a future bodily resurrection could hardly receive a more direct contradiction than is contained in this conversation, seeing that the only question was that of a future existence at all. The Sadducees cared nothing about the marriage relation in heaven, they denied immortality *in toto*, and to this denial the Saviour answers with consummate skill and gentleness, as was his wont.

In the account of this conversation which is given by Luke (xx., 37), we have the statement in this form: "Now that the dead are raised, even Moses showed at the bush, when he called the Lord the God of Abraham, and the God of Isaac, and the God of Jacob, for he is not the God of the

---

Sadducees, who say there is no resurrection,' *me einsi anastasin*—that there is no future state or no future existence for mankind. They ask, 'whose wife shall she be in the resurrection?' *en te anastasei*—in the future state. Our Saviour answers 'in the resurrection,' or as it should be translated, in the future state, . . . 'they are as the angels of God in heaven.' . . . 'Have ye not read that which was spoken unto you by God, concerning the future existence of those who are dead?' . . . This passage settles the dispute forever. Those who die, therefore, live after they are dead, and the future life is the *anastasis*, which is proven by our Saviour in this passage, and *which is universally denoted by this term throughout the New Testament*"!

dead, but of the living, for all live unto him;" and the argument is irresistible—God is not the God of dead men, but of living men; therefore, these patriarchs are alive now. There is not the least intimation here that their souls, as only a part of them, are living, but the entire man lives. In addition to the syllogistic argument, so conclusive as to the present living of these noted men, it is worthy of notice that the verb used is much more significant in this connection than the verbal form *anastasis* would be. It is the verb *egeiro*, whose primary application is to something already raised or aroused—the dead are raised, not will be hereafter.

The account given by Mark is in another form (xii., 26), yet it teaches the same doctrine exactly: "As touching the dead, that *they rise*"—not that they shall rise in some far off future, using the same verb, *egeiro*. The lesson is umistakable. *They are risen*, that is, they live. The dead continue to live nothwithstanding they pass through what we call death.

The account given by Matthew (xxii., 31), is still in another form teaching the same truth: "As touching the resurrection of the dead, have ye not read that which was spoken unto you by God, saying, 'I am the God of Abraham, and the God of Isaac, and the God of Jacob'? God is not the God of the dead but of the living." No wonder that when the people heard this they were astonished at his method of teaching. Here was a syllogism to prove the present living of these patriarchs, of whom their biographers had said, "They were gathered to their fathers," when mention was made of that change which men call death. They were alive at the time of Moses, said Christ; if alive then, they are alive now; therefore, there *is* an *anastasis*, a future life; a spirit life, and these men are now living it, *men*, not ghosts or souls, as a part of themselves, but real MEN!

Nothing could be more conclusive against the tradition of that age (that the bodies of men are to be gathered from the dust of ages,) than this refutation of the annihilationism of the Sadducees. As we have seen, Christ uses the word "resurrection" in its legitimate sense, as referring to a future existence, without giving countenance to the vagaries of the Pharisees any more than he meant to locate hell in the valley of the Sons of Hinnom when he used the word of the times in speaking of it.

The lesson, therefore, of this conversation with these unbelievers is this: By your own admissions you believe that God appeared to Moses in the bush. If he did, he announced himself as the God of the patriarchs who had died long before that time. But God is not a God of dead men, but of the living; therefore, Abraham, and Isaac, and Jacob were living when God spoke to Moses. If living then, they are living still; hence there is a resurrection, a *standing up again* of the dead, a future life—and that without any reference to bodies which, like those of these living patriarchs, have perished in the earth.

The argument would have been quite different if he had intended to countenance the notion of a future general resurrection of the material bodies. It would have run about thus: Ye do greatly err, not understanding the precise nature of that future life. Only the souls of men go directly to hell or heaven at death; but at the end of the world, which will be many thousand years hence, the bodies of all men and women will come forth from the graves, and from the seas, and from the flames, and from the flesh of the beasts of prey, and, emasculated by the omission of the sexual organs, so as to adapt them to a country where these organs will not be needed, they will be united with the long-separated souls—and then heaven or hell will be complete. Instead of such an admission, he neither here nor elsewhere gives any countenance to the idea of such a general resurrection.

It may be asked why the Saviour did not more directly disabuse the minds of the people on the subject of the future resurrection of the bodies of men if they were in error. We answer that he took every possible means to do so, as directly, and as explicitly, and as frequently, as he did to correct their notions concerning the nature of his mission—and with better results, as we shall see; for the apostles never preached a future general resurrection of the bodies of men, while to the last they expected a temporal kingdom to be set up.

There is much instruction on this subject in the account of the rich man and Lazarus. Lazarus died. No doubt his body was disposed of as were the bodies of other beggars, yet the account says *he* was carried by angels into Abraham's bosom. There was pomp and ceremony in disposing of the body of the rich man, yet "in hell *he* lifted up his eyes, being in torment, and seeth Abraham afar off and Lazarus in his bosom." The lesson to be learned from this narrative is every way an important one. In the first place it is introduced as a historic fact, not as a parable. There was a rich man and there was a beggar, they lived and died as here stated, and in the resurrection—in the *anastasis*, in the future life—one was happy, the other tormented, as here described. There is, however, no allusion here to the souls or ghosts of these men as only a part of themselves. Divested of all their earthly bodies, *they* appear, in the land of immortality, distinct and individual persons. Though one was happy and the other tormented, they could recognize each other and speak with each other. They had eyes and ears and tongues, though they had no material bodies; the spirit body is not to be without such members. The veritable Abraham was there, and the veritable Lazarus and the veritable rich man—all that appertained to the individuality of either; and all this, while their respective bodies were commingling with their mother earth.

While Jesus was engaged in his duties as a teacher on the eastern shore of the Jordan, his friend Lazarus, of Bethany, sickened and died. Soon afterwards the Master was found with the bereaved sisters, and in answer to a half-reproachful suggestion of Martha, he says: "Thy brother shall rise again," conveying much more meaning than a mere reference to the miracle he was about to perform; hence, he uses the word *anistemi*, referring to the after life, the genuine *anastasis*, conforming his meaning to the simile used with his disciples when he said that Lazarus slept. Martha comprehended this only within the limitations of her education, and answered accordingly, that she knew he should live again in the *anastasis*, in the world to come, or in the future life; but that would hardly relieve her present bereavement, for her faith postponed that event to some far off future, and probably referred to the popular belief in the revival of the body itself.

The tenderness and sympathy of the Saviour

were not more manifest in the tears which he shed at the grave, and in his benevolent act in restoring the lost brother, than in the gentle manner in which he proceeded to correct her mistake concerning the mode of man's immortality. It was no time for controversy nor for such a logical argument as he used with the Sadducees; hence, instead of ministering the comfort which that dogma is supposed to contain, by referring to the glories of the resurrection morn, as those who believe in a future physical resurrection are wont to do on such an occasion, he says, with a heart all overflowing with love: "Martha, I *am* the resurrection and the life: he that believeth in me, though he were dead, yet shall he live, and whosoever liveth and believeth in me *shall never die*." How could he, in other language, have so comprehensively stated the truth which eternally antagonizes Martha's creed and the materialism of the Pharisees? No wonder, therefore, that he asked from her a confession of faith in him as being what he here represents himself. How simple and confiding her answer: "I believe that thou art the Christ, the Son of God, which should come into the world."

To evade the force of this plain declaration of truth, those who would make Christ teach the doctrine of a future bodily resurrection make him say: "Shall never die eternally," whereas he said nothing at all about eternal death. His is simply a declaration of that underlying truth of Christianity, which attributes our immortality to Christ, the Redeemer, and which he states in other words to his disciples when he says, "Because I live, ye shall live also;" and still again when he says: "I am the way, the truth and the life."

Using the word resurrection in the sense that

he did when talking with the Sadducees, he here declares himself the source of that continuous life which is such that, though a man die, he continues to live; though he were dead, yet shall he live; and believing on him, the source of life, he does not die, but laying off this mortal, he at once puts on the immortal; ceasing to live on earth, among men, he lives in heaven, among the just made perfect.

The whole of these tender words were intended to correct the notion which Martha entertained in reference to that far-off resurrection at some last day, and to bring her to realize that what she called death was only a change from one mode of life to another, and to assure her that life is continuous and eternal.*

It is not an argument against this interpretation to say that no mention is here made of the immortality of those who do not believe in Christ. To press such an argument is to give color to the dogma of the annihilation of the wicked; for, if their immortality is here denied by such an omission, it is much more denied elsewhere.

The transfiguration of Christ teaches the same lesson. With disciples chosen for the occasion,

---

* The late Bishop Clark, whose scriptural arguments so often refute the creed which he writes to establish, in his book, *Man all Immortal*, says: "'Because I live, ye shall live also' *is the great pledge of our uninterrupted life. He that believeth hath eternal life; he that liveth and believeth on Him shall never die, and he that hath the Son hath life.* Christ is the source of our life, and as the source can not become extinct, neither can the life that flows from it. Death has no power here. Instead of locking our faculties up in unconsciousness, and isolating us from our union with Christ, it can only break down some of the obstructions to that intercourse that have heretofore existed.

"'O glorious hope of immortality!
At thought of thee, the coffin and the tomb
Affright no more, and e'en the monster, Death,
Loses his fearful form, and seems a friend.'"

he went up into a mountain, apart from the multitude. The scene which took place was one of transcendent beauty and glory. In describing it, the apostles use only superlatives, and yet seem to labor in vain to give us an adequate idea of the reality. Of the person of Christ they say: "His face did shine as the sun, and the fashion of his countenance was altered." Of his raiment they say: "It was white as the light, shining exceeding white as snow, so as no fuller on earth could white it, white and glistering."

Was the transformation anything else than laying aside, for the occasion, the *form* of a servant, which he had assumed when he divested himself of the *form* of God to undertake man's redemption? Peter afterwards calls the mountain the "mountain of glory," and Paul alludes to Christ's body as there seen, as "his body of glory," like to which ours shall be when mortality is swallowed up in life.

The thoughtful scholar cannot fail to connect this scene with another witnessed by John, many years afterwards, on the island of Patmos. There appeared amidst the golden candlesticks, "one like unto the Son of Man," yet so unlike the Man of Sorrows whom he had once followed, that he did not recognize him until the apparition introduced himself as "He who liveth and was dead, the Alpha and Omega." John says: "His head and his hairs were white like wool, as white as snow, and his eyes were as a flame of fire, and his feet like unto brass, as if they burned in a furnace."

No painter can transfer this picture to canvas, nor can any words give us any clearer idea of the reality; yet the Scriptures give us a personal interest in it, because it was to bring us to such a glory that the Captain of our salvation was made perfect through sufferings; for when we see him we shall be like him—pure spirit, having the image of God, as our first parents had before a body was formed for them of the dust of the ground.

At the transfiguration there were with him Moses and Elias, and they were like him in their appearance. And who were they? One was a prophet of olden times, who, after serving his generation, left the world in an unusual manner. Walking alone with his servant, Elisha, his body ascended, dropping only his outer mantle. What became of that body and the rest of the clothing he was wearing is merely a matter of conjecture. Those who believe in a literal resurrection of the bodies of men assume that somewhere in mid-air it was changed from a vile human form into a glorious, immortal and spiritual body, such as they suppose mortals will wear after the gathering up of the matter which once composed their earthly bodies.

Possibly this may be true. If the Omnipotent, who could create man a pure spirit in his own image and likeness before he formed a body for him out of earthy matter, now needs this earthly matter, or any part of it, as material out of which to make a spiritual body, this was probably the case. To us it seems much more scriptural and rational to suppose that the matter of Elijah's body, like the clothes it wore, was decomposed by natural causes, and found its way to mother earth as all other bodies do, and that the soul, *the man*, the real Elijah, appeared in heaven, with Abraham, Isaac, Jacob, David, Samuel, and other men, in his spiritual body; that is, a pure spirit, "as the angels of

God in heaven." Be this as it may, Elijah appeared with Christ, the veritable Elijah of history; not his ghost or spirit as only a part of him, and certainly not waiting for a future resurrection for the completion of his heavenly person.

"O certainly not," says the believer in a bodily resurrection; "he took his body up with him, and that body was spiritualized and glorified; and in a spiritual body thus prepared, he appeared with Christ." Very well; but how about Moses? Moses was not translated. He was certainly buried (very much as we suppose Elijah was). How came he to have a resurrection body—a spiritual body—a glorified body? He certainly made the same appearance as Elijah. Had some body-snatching angel been disturbing the repose of his dust in advance of Gabriel? This must have been the case if our complete equipment for immortality depends upon a reunion of soul and body after death. But does any one believe that the body of Moses was thus disturbed? Is it not still in the valley of Moab over against Beth-peor? If not, why not?

Is it not the dictate of good sense, as well as of sound faith, to believe the record just as it stands? *Two men* appeared in their heavenly forms, in their "spiritual bodies," in that "building of God," that "house not made with hands," "as the angels of God," "like Christ" in his transfigured body, his body of glory, just as all the just made perfect are like him when they see him *as he is*—neither of the two having any precedence over the other, although there is a difference in the general notion concerning their respective deaths and burials. They and the transfigured body of Christ were visible to the eyes of the disciples just as the chariots of Israel and the horsemen thereof were visible to the astonished servant of Elisha. No theory consistent with a future general resurrection can allow this, while the plain Bible doctrine of the mode of man's immortality allows it as entirely consistent with a thousand other facts in spiritual phenomena. The transaction is only another illustration of the continued existence of man, without regard to the body, whether, for sufficient reason, that be caught up in a chariot of fire, or be buried by the hand of God, or that of man.

But for the necessity of stripping this incident of its beauty in order to maintain the tradition of a bodily resurrection, it would have been hailed in all ages as one of the facts of the Gospel which bring to light life and immortality. More honorable in its associations than the interview between Saul and Samuel, it would, like that, have taught us how man continues to live after he is separated from his temporary earthly encumbrance.

The Saviour evidently intended to teach the same lesson in his conversation with the penitent thief upon the cross. The narrative is short, but it is full of meaning: "This day shalt *thou* be with *me* in paradise." As in all other cases, there is here no separation of the man into parts, sending one part to some half-way house to wait through interminable ages for a resurrection of the other part. Christ never gave any countenance to such a dogma. Then, if ever, he might be expected to; but he speaks to the *man*, of the *man*, and says, This day shalt *thou*, thy personality, thy real self, be with *me*, my real self, not in some underground cavern, but in paradise, in heaven. Here Christ is again teaching the continued personal existence of man in spite of that incident which we call death. There is to be no lapse of time between death and the possession of the fruition of immortality. No sophistry can evade the force of this lesson.

Taken together with the other incidents of the Crucifixion, the dying expression of the Saviour—"Father, into thy hands I commend my spirit"—casts no little light upon the mode of man's immortality. It was the spirit, the real man, escaping from the material form, and entering at once into the society of the Father. It was to be accompanied by the personality of the thief, to the home and presence of God. The thief was to go at once to paradise. The spirit of Christ, the immortal man, was to go to the hands of the Father; yet, they were to go together! Where is there in all this any place or time for the abode of Christ in some intermediate cavern or place, which was neither heaven nor earth, to be called *Sheol* or *Hades*, for thirty-six hours or more, before he should return to reanimate the lifeless clay which had been committed to Joseph's tomb? The Bible and the philosophical theory of man's immortality obviate all the confusion and absurdity which usually cluster around this closing scene, by assuming that the soul, the spirit, the real man, left the body, to feel no more interest in it than in any of the other particles of matter which had been taken on and thrown off during the third of a century past. The presence of God and paradise are one and the same—they are heaven. That the dying thief went thus to the society of the Father with the Saviour is evidence indisputable that we too, dying, shall be at once and forever with the Lord.

CHAPTER VII.

The Resurrection of Christ.

IN view of the vast importance which attaches to the resurrection of Christ, Peter might well say, "Blessed be the God and Father of our Lord Jesus Christ, which hath begotten us again unto a lively hope by the resurrection of Jesus Christ from the dead." It was henceforth to become the central fact in Gospel history, and one to which the Apostles never failed to appeal in their preachings, whether their audience were Jew or Gentile. Had this Man of many miracles and of matchless speech yielded to the dominion of death, that would have been an end of his authority and power. It was needful, therefore, that this final attestation of his mission should be, like the works which testify of him, public and indisputable.

His miracles were not wrought in a corner, and his resurrection was so public, and so well authenticated, that the apostles never attempted to prove it in their discourses to the Jews, but always alluded to it as an event which the Jews dared not deny. Human ingenuity could not have devised stronger proofs than human malice planned. Taken from the garden where he would have laid down his life of himself, all alone with his disciples, he was "lifted up," that the representatives of all nations, then thronging Jerusalem, might see that he died. That the most careless stranger in all that surging multitude might be attracted to the sufferer, there was written an "accusation" which could not fail to elicit notice, and it was written in every language which was spoken by that cosmopolitan crowd.

All this on the part of his enemies, while the Father called attention to the dying Son by the unnatural darkness and the earthquake. He had certainly died, and he was buried, and again human malice interposes to do what human ingenuity could not. The tomb was guarded by a band of men in the interest of his enemies, so as to prevent the possibility of a fraud; but, in spite of all this, he came forth from the grave, no less to the surprise of his disciples than of his enemies; but to the disciples it was the begetting of a lively hope, while to his enemies it became the fact in the history of Christ which they most had to dread. But, as we shall see, this resurrection had nothing to do with any future resurrection of man, and was never alluded to in that sense by the Apostles, but often referred to as a final and convincing attestation of authority and approval.

Of this resurrection we notice a few striking facts, as they stand out in the narrative. In the first place, the literal physical body of Christ came up out of the grave just as it had been laid there, three days before. To make this physical fact possible, the stone which had covered the grave was rolled away. What then became of the physical body, thus raised, we cannot tell.

It is very clear to our mind that none of the interviews had with the disciples were ever in that natural physical body. His challenge to Thomas does not necessarily indicate this. The disciples were alarmed at the sudden appearance, and they supposed they had seen a specter or a phantom. Dr. Strong renders the word *spirit* in the 37th verse, *apparition,* and in the 39th verse *spectre,* and the great Greek scholar, Griesbach, substitutes *phantasma* for *pneuma* in the text. It would be eminently appropriate for a man in the spirit form, "as an angel of God," to say that a phantom or specter had not flesh and bones such as the angels assumed when they talked and ate with Abraham and rescued Lot from the violence of the mob, and "such as you see me have." Elsewhere we quote from Dr. Whedon a very scriptural and rational opinion of the properties and capabilities of spirit, such as angels are. In his Notes on Luke xxiv., 29, he attributes to this person substantially the same attributes:

"Perhaps all will grant that our Lord's ordinary *stay* between the resurrection and ascension was in the invisible form. . . . His body possessed a superiority to the control of gravitation, to the need of food and clothing. . . . He was able, more or less, to modify it at will. . . . He could identify himself to Thomas; he could be grasped by the women; he could, like the angels in Gen. xxviii., 29, invest himself with apparent garments, and eat and drink before his disciples; [Then why not with *apparent* flesh and bones?] he could enter the invisible instantaneously; he could appear under 'another form,' could pass through any material impediments. . . . After his resurrection as at no previous time he seemed often unrecognizable to the best acquainted eyes. His ready presence at different places evinced his power of invisible and instantaneous transference through space at will."

Let it not be objected that if his appearances

were not in his real fleshly body then they were delusions. Not so, at all. His appearances were as real and in the same way as the angels at the tent of Abraham in the plains of Mamre, or as the angels to Lot in Sodom, and for as worthy a purpose. Those angels ate, and talked, and exerted physical strength, yet they were only angels in the form of men, if indeed they were not truly men, as the record states—some of the worthy ones who had lived in earlier years, returning, as afterwards Moses and Elijah did, to be ministering spirits to those heirs of salvation. Could not this incorporeal man now "as an angel of God" in like manner have assumed human shape, and even human flesh and bones as he indicated to Thomas? Even though he stood before his disciples clothed in veritable flesh and bones, as we cheerfully admit he did, it does not follow that it was the identical flesh and bones he had worn before death, any more than that the garments he appeared in were the identical garments which had been divided by lot and otherwise among the Roman soldiers. His eating and talking with his disciples do not prove that he carried about with him in a perpetually strange and unnatural manner the body which had been buried, and which had so certainly, yet so mysteriously, disappeared from the tomb. The extract from Dr. Whedon above quoted shows that he admits that if it were the veritable body it had been thoroughly spiritualized—deprived of every element of matter, as we understand matter, and clothed upon with every attribute of spirit, as nearly as we can comprehend spirit. In that better day of Scripture exegesis which is surely coming, and towards which the above quoted comment is a long stride as compared with the interpretation of former ages, the Christian church will discover nothing strange or inconsistent in any of the incidents recorded of the risen Saviour.

There are several circumstances which indicate that the appearances recorded were not in the real fleshly body. In the first place there is no case recorded in which the disciples or the women recognized him at first. Again, the record is almost uniformly in this manner: "He *appeared* first to Mary." "After that he *appeared* in *another form.*" "He *appeared* unto the eleven." "*Appeared* unto Simon." "And he *vanished* out of their sight."* He is represented as traveling rapidly, as entering rooms while the doors were shut and retiring in the same way, while it was necessary to roll away the stone from the door of the sepulchre that the real physical body might be removed. We repeat that no part of the narrative is consistent with the supposition that he "appeared" in his natural fleshly body. Where did he keep himself during the repeated interims between these "appearances?" Why was he seen only by chosen ones? Even on the occasion when he challenged inspection he had "appeared" suddenly, the doors being shut.

To suppose that the essential personality of the Saviour went at once to paradise, as he had promised, and as all do who die in the Lord, and that on the morning of the third day the angel,

* Some persons of average reading seem to regard this *vanishing* as nothing more than the *hiding* alluded to, John viii., 59. No modern commentator of repute so regards it. *Lange*, on John viii., 59, says: "A vanishing out of sight, as in Luke xxiv., 31, is hardly to be thought of." *Strong* says: "Jesus escaped by burying himself in the midst of the crowd." *Whedon* says: "Jesus probably moved away by a route which interposed protecting objects."

which had physical strength enough to roll away the great stone, had at the same time taken charge of the material remains of the Saviour and suitably disposed of them, as the body of Elijah and that of Moses had been disposed of, and that the several interviews were just what the evangelists represent them to have been—"appearances," sometimes in one form and sometimes in another, as they tell us—is to remove from the narrative inconsistencies and contradictions which tradition has thrown around it, and to make it consistent with itself, and with known laws of matter and of spirit.

In the disappearance of the body from the grave, under the circumstances, all was accomplished which the Divine Father had in view by its resurrection—an attestation of its mission. The facts of that disappearance were so public and so well authenticated that no appearance of the risen Christ was necessary, except to his disciples. The earthquake, and the power which felled the soldiers, and the testimony of the Roman guards themselves, convinced the Jews that it was no trick or fraud practiced by the disciples.

That the disciples understood these visits of the Saviour to be just what they call them, "appearances," is evident not only from the narratives of the four evangelists, but from the statement of Paul also. In his enumeration of the several times of these interviews, he says: "Last of all he was seen of me also." How? Certainly not in his physical body. Even those whose dogma needs the physical body of Christ to have gone through so many unnatural and *unphysical* performances, that they may have a "model" for their bodily resurrection, will not claim this;

for, according to their theory, that body had been spiritualized and glorified, and to have it now assume human form is all that we claim for Christ, as a spirit, on these occasions. Evidently, the appearance to Paul thus referred to was distinct from the vision which he had when, "in the body or out of the body," he was caught up to see the unutterable things of the future life, and was in like manner with the other appearances, and for the same purpose—to communicate important information in order to confirm him in the faith of the Gospel.*

Again, how different the account given of the risen Saviour and the risen Lazarus! Lazarus was seen by the whole people, foes as well as friends of Jesus, and the enemies of Christ counseled how they might put him to death also, when they should kill the Saviour. The narrative speaks of Lazarus as a living man, moving among the people as any other man; but there is not the least intimation of any such a man in the person of the risen Christ. He is utterly unknown to his enemies, and known only to a very few of his friends, and to them only on occasions chosen by him, not by them.†

---

* "He here, no doubt, speaks of Christ's appearing to him on the way to Damascus."—*Joseph Benson.*

"It is evident, from the history of Saul's conversion, that Jesus Christ did *appear* to him."—*Dr. Adam Clarke.*

† We here take the liberty of quoting a few paragraphs from the book "Credo," already alluded to, as showing that some of the sentiments above expressed are not merely the vagaries of an eccentric mind, and, therefore, to be dismissed with a dignified, pooh! pooh! but that men of recognized scholarship and high official position are abandoning the grooves of old exposition on this subject. Dr. Townsend, the author, is one of the most esteemed teachers in the Methodist Theological School at Boston, and, notwithstanding invectives have been hurled at him by less progressive thinkers, he is retained in a position best calculated to enable him to unsettle old

beliefs, and introduce new interpretations of the Scripture. If this does not give the sanction of that church to such opinions, it at least indicates the dawn of that day of Christian liberality which no longer puts men in theological straight-jackets, and requires a pronunciation of a given Shibboleth as a condition of fraternal recognition:

"The argument for the resurrection of the old body, particle for particle, is also supported, it is claimed, by the fact that Christ's natural body was the one raised from the tomb.

"Two suppositions are legitimately deduced from Christ's literal resurrection: either that it was designed to be a seal of his commission, a manifest miracle, to confirm the world of his divinity, to reassure the wavering faith of the disciples, and, being witnessed by more than five hundred different persons, to have vast influence in spreading Christianity during the first century, or else it was designed to be an exact type of our own resurrection.

"Which of these two suppositions is the more reasonable? Do the Scriptures by word or hint suggest that Christ's resurrection was a type of ours? Can his resurrection, in any proper sense, be an exact type? Were the most important conditions of such a resurrection fulfilled by him? He was but three days in the grave, while we must slumber there for ages. He did not see corruption, while we are to become dust and ashes. But even if this difficulty could be removed—though it can not—would it not seem far more reasonable, and infinitely more grand, to look upon our Saviour's resurrection as the seal of his divinity, and the first fruits, not of the resurrection, but of them that slept? Where, then, is Christ's physical body? it may be asked. Did it ascend to heaven? Did not the disciples witness its ascension? Is he not there to-day? Flesh and blood are not there. 'Five bleeding wounds he bears' is Watts' poetry, not Paul's Letter to the Corinthians. Christ's glorified body was not the body shown to Thomas. Save at the transfiguration, it was not seen by any of the disciples until after the ascension. It was then seen. Stephen saw it, crowned with dazzling splendor, on the day of his martyrdom. Paul saw it above the glory of the sun, on the road to Damascus. John saw it in Patmos. Great multitudes of dying Christians have seen it. Nay, we believe the valley is dark and lonely to him only who knows not Christ. But this glorious body is not precisely the one which walked to Emmaus, or met Mary at the tomb. Where is that body? We do not know where it is. The record says nothing about it, and beyond the record we can not go. We might say that the fleshly covering was annihilated, or that it underwent a gradual transformation, or was cast off, and the gross materials flung back to earth, but it is only *safe* to say that he has a glorious body, which is now the type of our resurrection body, without flesh, without blood. . . May we not, then, conclude that Christ's resurrection was designed for a seal of his ministry, rather than an exact type of our resurrection?"—*Credo, page* 307.

We add, parenthetically, that, though neither Dr. Townsend nor Dr. Whedon adopts fully our exposition, they both repudiate the old notion, and by that much at least prepare the way for the adoption of a more rational and scriptural theory. They each go as far as it is prudent for them to go, seeing the official relation which they sustain to the dogma of a general resurrection of some kind at the end of the world, though on that subject they differ radically from each other, and each from the common opinion.

CHAPTER VIII.

The Teachings of the Apostles on the Resurrection.

WE ought to find the doctrine of the future general resurrection of the bodies of men in the sermons of the Apostles, if they ever believed or taught any such thing. Let us carefully examine the few specimen sermons which have come down to us. While in them we shall find abundance of Jesus and *the* Resurrection, we will not find one word or syllable which can be properly construed into that figment of dogmatic theology which is commonly known as the general resurrection.

In the 18th verse of the seventeenth chapter of the Acts, we find a statement of the impression which Paul's preaching made upon certain Grecian philosophers at Athens, and they accused him of being a setter-forth of strange gods, and therefore the introducer of a new religion. The feature of his discourse which was most striking to them was that he preached Jesus and the resurrection. They demanded an explanation of this and he proceeded to give it, first by a reference to their own beliefs and poets, and then, lifting them higher by their acknowledged views of the true God, he insisted that such a God could not be made of silver or gold, after man's device. This true God, said he, has heretofore winked at the times of ignorance, but now he commandeth all men everywhere to repent, "for he hath appointed a day [not necessarily just 24 hours long] in which he will judge the world in righteousness by that man whom he hath ordained." "How shall we know that? What assurance can be given of such a truth?" the Athenian was ready to inquire. To which Paul replies: "Of this he hath given assurance unto all men, in that he hath raised him from the dead." That this is *the* resurrection which caused the talk, and is alluded to in the 18th verse, is clear from what follows in the next verse: "And when they heard of the resurrection of the dead, some mocked." Of what dead? So far as the record states, or any inference can be drawn from it, there had been no reference to any dead but the dead Christ. Even if these scoffers should have alleged that he taught a general resurrection of all the dead, or any number of the dead, that would be no proof that he did so teach, for they had just lied against him in charging that he taught that Jesus was a king, opposed to Cæsar (verse 7).

But it is not plain that even their language can be tortured to mean all this. He had introduced the resurrection of Christ only as an *assurance* of his right to judge the world. He refers to the same resurrection in Romans (i., 14) for the same purpose: "He was made of the seed of Abraham according to the flesh, but by *his resurrection from the dead* he was *declared to be the Son of God* with power. Again, in the same spirit, and for the same purpose, he refers to this great fact when explaining Christ to his Hebrew brethren at Antioch: "We declare to you glad tidings . . how that God hath fulfilled the same to us in that he hath raised up Jesus again." Acts xiii., 33.

Is there any future general resurrection, or any other future resurrection, in any of these? Language could not more definitely fix it, than as it is here limited to the resurrection of the dead Christ, and this is not argued, nor even asserted, but it is alluded to, as a well known fact, only as an "assurance" that Jesus had been appointed by the Father to "judge the world in righteousness."

In the twenty-sixth chapter we have another sermon in which this favorite theme is discussed. The sixth verse reads thus: "And now I stand and am judged for the hope of the promise made of God unto the fathers." What promise? Certainly not the promise of a future general resurrection, for no such a promise was ever made. Take your reference Bible, and you will be pointed to such passages as these: 2 Sam., vii., 12, "When thy days shall be fulfilled, and thou shalt sleep with thy fathers, I will set up thy seed after thee." Ps. cxxxii., 11: "The Lord hath sworn unto David, of the fruit of thy body I will set upon thy throne." Isaiah vii., 14, "Behold, a virgin shall conceive and bear a son, and shall call his name Emmanuel"—and much more of like import.

This was the promise made of God to the Fathers, and when we read these promises we do not so much wonder that the Jews expected a temporal deliverer; and when we find the Apostles so often referring to this hope, so long after the death of Christ, we will not wonder that they tinged their faith still with a hope of his return during their own lives, or, at furthest, during that generation, to fulfill this promise, as we shall see by and by.

"It is for the sake of this hope, King Agrippa,

that I am accused of the Jews," said the Apostle. But Christ had died; how, then, could this hope yet remain? Why, it depended upon his resurrection from the dead; hence the constant coupling of this fact with the hope, and it was this which gave the offense. His appeal to Agrippa's knowledge of the true God, though a Gentile, has no other significance than this. He asks: "Why should it be thought a thing incredible with you that God should raise the dead?" What dead? Certainly not the *bodies* of all the dead, at some remote future time, but the dead Christ. True enough, the Greek adjective is plural, but that does not prove that he meant to include the dead bodies of all men. It is only a common form of stating a general proposition, which may be applicable to only one person. Thus, we may be speaking of the exercise of some executive pardon which excites surprise. Should we reply by asking: "Do you think it strange that the Governor should pardon criminals?" we should not expect to be understood that the Governor had pardoned all the criminals, or that he ever would. The question would be just as appropriate if he had never pardoned but the one, and never was expected to pardon another.

Read Paul's touching allusion to his own personal experience, beginning at a time when he was no more of a believer than Agrippa, and ending with a statement of the doctrine of his several sermons, in this language: "Having obtained help of God, I continued unto this day, witnessing to both small and great, saying *none other things* than these which the prophets and Moses did say should come: *That Christ should suffer, and that he should be the first that should rise from the dead*, and should .show light unto the people and to the Gentiles."

We have here Paul's own declaration that he never preached a future resurrection of the bodies of men, for he preached *none other things* than those here enumerated. Again, take your reference Bible and look up the sayings of Moses and the prophets, from which it is assumed that Paul preached a future general resurrection, and you will find no such resurrection in or near them. His appeal to Agrippa, a Gentile, as a believer in the prophets, is a beautiful specimen of eloquence, but utterly meaningless if he had had any reference to such a doctrine, because that doctrine is not in the prophets.

It will be observed that this final statement of the manner and matter of his preaching is the summing up of his defense, as it had been made several times in the course of his trial, which had now lasted over two years, and which had begun before the Chief Captain (chap. xxi., 37). Before the Council, consisting of both Sadducees and Pharisees (chap. xxiii., 6), Paul states that he is called in question for the hope *and* the resurrection of the dead. What that hope and that resurrection were we have already seen. He evidently uses the word *resurrection* here in its generic sense, just as Christ did in his conversation with the Sadducees, as intending to antagonize the doctrine of that sect; and the author of the record so applies and so explains it, for he tells us just what the Sadducees meant by their creed: "no resurrection" [no future life], for they believed in "neither angel nor spirit"; but the Pharisees believed in a resurrection, that is in a future life, for they "confessed both," angel and spirit.

He repeats the same, substantially, before Felix (chap. xxiv., 14): "I confess that after the way which they call heresy, so worship I the God of my fathers, believing all things which were written in the law and the prophets, and have hope towards God, which they themselves allow, that there shall be a resurrection of the dead, both of the just and the unjust."

Here is a beautiful coupling of his faith in the resurrection, that is, in a future life, with the doctrines of Christ as they had been foretold by the prophets; how he should suffer and rise from the dead. Using the word resurrection in the sense that Christ used it when disputing with the Sadducees, as referring to the future life, and as it is everywhere used in the Bible, except when specifically applied to Christ, he gives no countenance to the doctrines of the reanimation of dead bodies at some far future time.

Putting the accusation and the defense together, we have this statement: In chapter xxiv., 21, he says: "Touching the resurrection of the dead I am called in question." In explaining how he preached the resurrection of the dead, he informs us, two years afterwards, in the twenty-sixth chapter, that it was by saying "none other things . . . *than that Christ should suffer and that he should be the first that should rise from the dead.*"

At another time we find Paul preaching this same resurrection to the Thessalonians. The report of that sermon will be found in the seventeenth chapter, 3d verse: "That Christ must needs have suffered and risen again from the dead." No general resurrection at the last day here!

In the twenty-fifth chapter we have a scrap of history such as would be considered very valuable in any legal investigation where circumstantial evidence might be needed; (though, in fact, we are not in need of mere circumstantial evidence, having direct proof enough that *the* resurrection which was preached by Paul referred wholly to Christ, except where the context plainly shows a reference to the doctrine of the *anastasis*, or immortality, as contrasted with the annihilationism of the Sadducees.)

Paul had been before Festus, accused by the Jews of many grievous things. During his preliminary trial, as is well said by Dr. Whedon in his notes on the 19th verse: "Jesus and the resurrection had evidently been debated." The impression made upon the mind of Festus by Paul's method of preaching this doctrine is thus given in his statement of the charge brought against Paul. "They had certain questions against him of their own superstition, and of one Jesus which was dead, *whom Paul affirmed to be alive.*" Here we have, in a semi-official form, that in preaching *the* resurrection he preached *that Jesus was alive.* Nothing more. Not one word about a general resurrection.

We have thus followed Paul through his sermons and found not a shadow of a general resurrection at the last day. Let us turn to Peter's sermons, a few of which are preserved.

On the day of Pentecost he says: "Him, being delivered by the determined counsel and foreknowledge of God, ye have taken, and with wicked hands, have crucified and slain, whom God *hath raised up.* (Acts ii, 23.)

In the thirty-second verse he repeats the same doctrine, thus: "This Jesus *hath God raised up.*"

In the third chapter, at the fourteenth verse,

he recurs to his favorite theme, Jesus and the resurrection, in this manner: "But ye denied the holy one and the just, and killed the Prince of Life *whom God hath raised from the dead.*"

In the twenty-sixth verse he preached *the resurrection of the dead* in a manner which grieved the Sadducees, and they laid hands on him and put him in prison on that account. And here is the sermon: "*God having raised up Jesus* sent him to bless you." There is not a word of allusion to any other resurrection than that of Christ in this sermon or in any that preceded it.

In his defense, which followed (chap. iv., 10), he does not apologize and say that they misunderstood him and therefore misrepresented him, but he defiantly repeats the doctrine of the *resurrection of the dead* in these words: "Be it known unto you all, and to all the people of Israel, that by the name of Jesus Christ, whom ye crucified, *whom God raised from the dead*, by him doth this man stand before you whole."

In the fourth chapter, at the twenty-third verse, we have a summary of the preaching of the apostolic band, and its results, in these significant words: "And with great power gave the apostles witness of *the resurrection of the Lord Jesus Christ*, and great grace was on them all."

Subsequently, having been released from prison by the ministry of an angel, the apostles were found preaching in the temple, "all the words of this life." Surely here we shall find the resurrection of the bodies of all men, at some future time, as connected with the pattern which Christ set in his resurrection, as a fulfillment of the pledge which the resurrection of Christ gave, for they preached "all the words of this life." But here is all that the historian thought it necessary to record: "*The God of our fathers raised up Jesus,* whom ye slew and hanged upon the tree. Him hath God exalted to be a prince and a Saviour, to give repentance to Israel and the remission of sins."

This, then, was apostolic preaching as shown in the book of the Acts. They preached repentance and the remission of sins, through the name of the Lord Jesus, and alluded constantly to the resurrection of Christ as an "assurance" that God had constituted him a prince and a Saviour, never once speaking of the resurrection of the bodies of all men as any part of the scheme of salvation. They speak of the future life of man as connected with the sacrifice of Christ—a resurrection—a future life of the just and the unjust. Enough, also, is recorded to show that they still expected a fulfillment of "the promise to the fathers," a restoration of the nation of the Jews to prosperity and power—a lingering Jewish error which tinged all their writings and sermons, as we shall see in the proper place.

CHAPTER IX.

CHRIST'S DIRECT TEACHING OF THE TIME AND MODE OF MAN'S IMMORTALITY.

HAVING thus examined the matter and manner of apostolic preaching, we recur to the more direct teaching of the Saviour on this subject to show that these disciples did not depart from rightful authority in attributing human immortality to the merits of Christ. It is only through Christ that man lives—Christ the resurrection and the life.

On the occasion of the miracle which healed the impotent man, recorded in the fifth chapter of John, the Saviour more distinctly declares his character and mission than he ever had before, if not more distinctly than at any other time whatever, giving additional offense to the Jews, who had been outraged by his healing on the Sabbath. His announcement of his divinity is conclusive, unless we assume that he willingly left them in error concerning the import of his language. His account of himself is about this: "Whatsoever the Father doeth, the Son doeth likewise. I have healed a sick man, and ye marvel. There are greater works committed to the Son than this. As the Father raiseth up the dead and quickeneth them, even so the Son quickeneth whom he will. He that heareth my words and believeth on Him that sent me, hath everlasting life, and shall not come into condemnation because he hath passed from death unto life. Verily, verily, I say unto you, that the hour is coming, *and now is*, when the dead shall hear the voice of the Son of God, and they that hear shall live."

In the twenty-eighth verse the expression is somewhat different, chiefly in using the word *graves*, and in omitting the phrase *now is*. The usual method of disposing of these passages is to make the twenty-fifth verse refer to a spiritual resurrection, but the twenty-eighth to the general resurrection of bodies at the end of the world. Dr. Whedon perhaps as correctly expresses the opinion of those who find a bodily resurrection here as any other writer, when he says: "*All that are in their graves.* It is *universal*, ALL. It is bodily, and of the same body that was buried. The very *bodies* that are laid in the graves are the bodies that arise. The very body that dies is the body that revives." This is the germ thought, the central idea of the doctrine of a bodily resurrection—"The very body that dies is the body that revives," and this passage, more than all other passages of Scripture, is relied upon to prove it.

Let us examine it a moment. The language is: "All that are in their graves shall hear his voice and shall come forth." But this does not say all the *bodies* that are in the graves shall come forth. Whatever it refers to is predicated of the entire man. It is repugnant to every sentiment of Christianity, and no less to half-enlightened heathenism, to locate our departed ones in the grave, and it is sheer pettifogging to say that because only the body goes into the grave, therefore, Christ referred only to the body. Will any intelligent Christian say that if Christ were speaking of Abraham, and Isaac, and Jacob he would locate them in their graves? When he spoke of them he spoke of them as living, not as dead. If Christ had intended to teach the doctrine of a resurrection of bodies he would not have spoken of the entire man as being in the grave, but would have said, as he nowhere says or intimates: that the *bodies* which are in the graves shall hear his voice and shall come forth. Again: whatever or whoever are here intended could hear. Dead *bodies* cannot hear any more than rocks can hear, and it is forcing a meaning upon Christ's words that is unauthorized to say that when he chooses he can make rocks or dust hear. The simple natural truth is that he uses the words "in the graves" just as we use the words often. We say "he has gone to his grave," or "he is in his grave," meaning only that he is dead. Hence the discovery that quite another thing is meant by the 28th verse from that implied in the 25th is wholly gratuitous and unauthorized. This is further evident, because, if the words are not used in this sense, none are to be raised unless they have been literally buried.

But even if the language were as emphatic as the language of Dr. Whedon above quoted, and taught a bodily resurrection as unmistakably, it would be inadmissible to prove such a doctrine as that of a reanimation of the scattered dust of the millions who have died in the ages past, and the millions yet to die in the millions of years yet to come, by this one Scripture, especially when it stands as this does, in the midst of such Scriptures as these: "He that believeth on me, out of his belly shall flow rivers of living water." Why may we reject the plain grammatical meaning of this text, which teaches such a physical impossibility, and yet must accept as literal that which refers to the dead, even supposing that he refers to bodies only? This is not a whit more impracticable or improbable than that. The only difference is that we know this is not true, by daily observation; we are not allowed to exercise our senses, or to reason on the other, because we are told it is outside the realm of reason, and purely within the realm of faith.

Again: why may we refuse to accept the literal meaning of this other passage, all in close connection with the one on which so much stress is laid: "Except ye eat the flesh of the Son of Man and drink his blood ye have no life in you. Whoso eateth my flesh and drinketh my blood hath eternal life, and I will raise him up at the last day," and not be permitted to suggest that the former may have some other than its literal meaning,—even if the Saviour had said: "I will raise up the bodies which are in the graves," which he does not? This verse just quoted has also resurrection in it—resurrection at the last day at that, but it is a resurrection which cannot take place unless we eat the flesh and drink the blood of Christ. The Papists find transubstantiation in this text, Protestants do not. The Papists prove their doctrine by it with much less circumlocution than the doctrine of a bodily resurrection can be proven from the former.

By the exercise of that plain common sense which educes from the hyperbolic passages we have just quoted some of the most cheering and instructive doctrines of the Bible, these two companion texts, and several of like import scattered among these figurative declarations of the Saviour, can be made to harmonize with the other teachings of the word, and to convey truths of the utmost moment; but a bodily resurrection is in neither of them.

Whatever is predicated of one is of the other. The phrase, *In the graves* means the same as *the dead*, and nothing more. What then is taught? It is something that *now is*. The use of the present tense is significant. The Father *raiseth;* the Father *quickeneth;* the Father *judgeth;* he that *heareth; believeth; is passed; hath committed.* The import of the whole is that, since the Father hath committed all judgment to the Son, and the Son hath life in himself, from this time forward the dead shall hear the voice of the Son of God, and they that hear shall live, and he will exercise his authority as judge to separate the righteous from the wicked, just as, from the beginning until now, the Father hath quickened and judged.

Unquestionably, the raising up of the dead, the future life, and all that is implied in this marvelous demonstration of power, was something already begun, of which the curing of the impotent man was only an evidence of the right and power. Instead of intending to teach what is sometimes claimed of this conversation, it is really aimed at the prevailing materialism of the times, just as his conversations with the Sadducees and with Martha were. The occasion was different, and the style is different, but the lesson is the same, and it is consistent with the general teaching of the Bible on the subject of man's immortality. The dying man hears the voice of the Son of God and lives; that is, immortality is through Christ, and now, not untold ages hence. To Martha he expressed this same truth when he said: "He that believeth on me shall never die." To these Jews, on this occasion, he says: "He that believeth on him that sent me *hath* everlasting life."

The import of his account of himself, given in the sixth chapter of John, is precisely the same as here. "The bread of God is he which cometh down from heaven and *giveth* life to the world. I *am* the bread of life. And this is the will of him that sent me, that every one that seeth the Son and believeth on him may have everlasting life, and I will raise him up at the last day." If what had preceded this expression had not definitely fixed the meaning of the phrase, "at the last day," as referring to the time of the man's death, what follows (verse 47) does: "Verily, Verily, I say unto you, he that believeth on me *hath everlasting life*." But, lest their tradi tional ideas of a future general resurrection might rob this doctrine of its beauty and force, he repeats—v. 50: "This is the bread which cometh down from heaven, that a man may eat thereof, *and not die*. . . . If any man eat of this bread, he shall live forever. . . . Whoso eateth my flesh and drinketh my blood *hath eternal life*, and I will raise him up at the last day."* (I will give him life when he comes to die.) And yet again, as though he would repeat this truth so that it never could be forgotten or misunder-

---

* The absurdity of predicating a closing up of terrestrial things upon this and similar phrases is manifest to any one who will explain Scripture by Scripture, with a purpose to reach the truth, instead of building up a dogma. Paul defines the end of the world in Hebrews ix., 26: "In the end of the world hath he appeared." He does the same, i Cor., x., 11: "For our admonition, upon whom the ends of the world have come." Peter, Acts ii., 17, defines the last days to be the days in which he lived; and Paul, Heb. i., 2, says "in these last days he hath spoken by his Son." There is not a well defined instance in which either phrase refers to the closing up of earth's history.

stood, he adds (v. 57): "As the living Father hath sent me, and I live by the Father, so he that eateth me, *even he shall live by me.* . . . He that eateth this bread *shall live forever.* . . . It is the spirit that *quickeneth.* . . . The words that I speak unto you, they are spirit, *and they are life.*"

One other passage, often quoted to prove the doctrine of a bodily resurrection, is found in Rev. xx., 13: "And the sea gave up the dead which were in it, and death and hell [*Hades*] delivered up the dead which were in them." But this can not be made to even allude to a bodily resurrection, without according to it its proper place in Biblical literature, that of high-wrought oriental poetry, and then as a proof text it wholly disappears.

The usual method of appropriating it is to assume that it refers to a general resurrection and then to prove that it refers to the bodies of men, "because neither Christian nor heathen ever believed that the souls of men go into the sea." Such expositors seem to wholly overlook the second clause of the text, which predicates the same thing of *Hades*, for it too delivers up the dead which are in it. We may ask quite as dogmatically: Does any one, Christian or heathen, ever believe that the *bodies* of men go into *Hades?* If universal belief is worth any thing in the first clause, it is equally valuable in the second. If *dead* means bodies when coming from the sea, why does it not mean bodies when coming from *Hades?* It is an unwarrantable species of argumentation to assume a doctrine, and then prove it by thus making the same word mean such dissimilar things in the same sentence. It means just what it says in each case—*the dead*, not the bodies as such, nor the souls as such, but *the dead*, and its meaning will be easily ascertained when we find the meaning of the other poetic language used in its immediate connection.

In the sensuous ages which found in this poem a literal great white throne, a literal recording angel, who kept a literal account with every man, in literal books; and that at a literal judgment these literal books were literally opened; that there was a literal camp of literal saints, and that a literal Gog and Magog surrounded the literal camp of these literal saints; and that there was a literal battle, and that the whole ended in locking up the discomfited in a literal lake of literal fire and literal brimstone—in such an age it was bearable that, as a part of the things here literally described, there should be a literal resurrection of the dead from the sea, and from death, and from *Hades;* but even then it was not allowable to prove a bodily resurrection unless the body went to Hades also, for it, too, gave up exactly what the sea gave up—nothing more and nothing less. But why should the lake, the fire, the brimstone, the great white throne, the camp, and the battle all be dismissed by intelligent expositors from the catalogue of literal things, and yet the resurrection and the judgment be retained; and then the text be mutilated to prove a resurrection of bodies in one clause, and a resurrection of souls or something else in another, though the same word is used in both? It cannot be allowed. There is no resurrection in the text at all, much less a resurrection of bodies, at the end of the world.

But if this view of the subject did not remove the text from any possible service in proof of a bodily resurrection, the fact that the sea holds, at any one time, a very insignificant fraction of the bodies of men, should indicate that so general and universal an event as the supposed final resurrection could be very imperfectly taught by such language. Allow that all who are drowned in any and all waters, whose bodies are not rescued and buried, and all who are buried in "the deep, deep sea," remain in the waters, it would still be too insignificant a fraction of the whole to demand such prominence; but the bodies which fall into the water, whether river, lake or ocean, remain in water but a short time, even in a disorganized state. If the monsters of the deep do not devour them, and thus give the matter which once composed those bodies new forms, and start it out on ten thousand subsequent destinies, the action of the waves brings the decomposed matter to the surface, and light, and heat, and winds, and clouds bear it to the neighboring forests and fields, just as all other gaseous matter is borne, and it becomes a part of trees and plants, the same as though it had perished on the land and remained unburied, or buried—for the deepest graves of only a quarter of a century contain but little that can be recognized as the dust once animated by a living man.

The sea gives up the dead bodies which are in it every day and every hour, by the law which God has ordained. Of all that is given to it, it retains nothing for any such final surrender as the theory of a general resurrection requires.

CHAPTER X.

THE ARGUMENT OF THE FIFTEENTH CHAPTER OF FIRST CORINTHIANS.

THE most elaborate and conclusive discussion of the mode of man's immortality, except in the conversations of Christ with the Sadducees, and with the enraged Jews, is found in the fifteenth chapter of First Corinthians. The immediate occasion of this was that some had been teaching that there *is no* resurrection of the dead. Paul does not allege that any one has been denying the doctrine of a future general resurrection, but they have denied that mode of immortality which the Saviour alluded to when he spoke of the continuous existence of the patriarchs; and Paul uses the word "resurrection" in the sense that Christ did, as applicable to the after-life which those patriarchs were already enjoying when God spoke of them to Moses.

This is the same heresy as that alluded to in 2d Tim. ii., 18. "Saying that the resurrection is past." It was that narrow view of the Christian religion which limited its benefits to this life only, and to the Hebrew people chiefly if not exclusively; a view entertained by nearly all Hebrew converts until after the destruction of the temple, some four years after this letter to Timothy. Paul himself was not wholly free from it until this last imprisonment, as we show elsewhere, though his faith was more comprehensive from the beginning than that of any other apostle; a fact which often led him into sharp controversies with the Judaïzing teachers. Hymeneus, and Alexander, and Philetus, had given him much trouble on this score, and he turned two of them over to Satan, that they might learn better, (1 Tim. i., 20,) and prayed rather an equivocal prayer for Alexander, (2 Tim. iv., 14,) showing the depth of his grief on account of their persistent denial of the doctrine of a future life through Christ.

The first part of this chapter (1 Cor. xv.,) is an argument in favor of a future life based upon the sacrifice and merits of Christ, that life whose resurrection was an "assurance" that God had ordained him for this purpose, (Acts xvii., 13,) with no reference whatever to the mode of attaining. The latter part is devoted to the mode, in answer to the fool who insisted on knowing with what body they would come, repeating, substantially, the materialistic objections of the Sadducees. In his answer, as we shall see, he uses almost every possible form of speech to assure the objector that he will not live in a material, fleshly body, but that he will live, notwithstanding; for Christ lives, and because he lives we shall live also.

He introduces his argument for man's immortality by referring to his method of preaching when, six years before that time, he established the church at Corinth. This reference to his manner of preaching shows that his theme was the same as when preaching among his own countrymen: "Jesus and the resurrection." "I delivered unto you first of all, that Christ died for our sins, according to the Scriptures, and that he was buried, and *that he rose again the third day*, according to the Scriptures." One cannot fail to notice the similarity of this account with that given to Agrippa: "Saying *none other things* than those which Moses and the prophets did say should come: that Christ should suffer, and that he *should be the first that should rise from the dead.*"

Only in one thing did his sermons in Greece differ from his sermons in Judæa. Here he never alluded to the evidences of Christ's resurrection; there he details the manner by which they became satisfied of its truth, but in neither account does he give any intimation that he ever preached a future general resurrection of the bodies of men.

Proceeding with his argument, he says: "Now, if Christ be preached that he rose from the dead, how say some among you that there *is* no resurrection of the dead?" (Not that there *will be* no resurrection, as would be proper if he had referred to a future general resurrection.) "But if there be no resurrection of the dead (no future life), then is Christ not risen, and our preaching is vain, and ye are yet in your sins, and they that have fallen asleep in Christ are perished."

This is a summing up of the terrible failure which would have befallen Christianity but for the "assurance" which the Father gave of the acceptability of the sacrifice of Christ, by raising him from the dead.

Having thus settled the preliminary fact that Christ had risen, he proceeds to say that in rising he became the first fruits of them that slept. Among the children of Israel the "first fruits" was an offering to God of the first sheaves of the harvest, the first grapes of the vintage, and the first of everything, including the first-born of the family or of the herd. It was a contribution to the expenses of religious worship; the first-born of the family and of unclean beasts being redeemed by something which could be made serviceable as food for the priesthood. Its significance was that God had the first claim upon their increase, as well as that the first was generally the best of its kind. The requirement is the antithesis of that which forbade the offering of the lame, and the deformed, and the imperfect,—the giving, grudgingly, after every other claim was satisfied, an offering to God. Just in what sense the apostle uses the figure here is not known. Quite likely it is in the sense which was most common at that time, as the best of its kind. Thus he uses it, Romans viii., 23: "But we have the first fruits of the spirit,"—the best gifts of the spirit, as the context clearly shows. James, chapter i., 18, uses it in the same sense when he calls Christians "a kind of first fruits of his creatures."

It may be equivalent to the phrase in Acts xxvi., 33: "The first that should rise from the dead," and it may mean that Christ was the first to rise from the dead with such public demonstrations as to confirm the truth of an after life. How public and convincing these were, he enumerates in the beginning of his argument. In Colossians i., 18, he calls Christ "the beginning, the *first-born* from the dead," and the same idea is used, Rev. i., 5, where he is called "the first-begotten of the dead." But, in whatever sense it may be used, there is no authority in the Bible for the interpretation which uses it in the sense of an earnest or pledge, or an example or pattern. The latter it could not be, for his body saw no corruption, and if the appearances which are recorded were his real fleshly body, it was all deformed by the wounds of the crucifixion.*

The entire argument of the first part of this chapter is to show that the resurrection of the dead, that *anastasis* which implies living hereafter, is a fundamental doctrine of Christianity, and that the Corinthians had been so instructed, and had so believed. To deny this doctrine now was to renounce everything which appertained to the

---

* A writer of some celebrity, in the Methodist *Quarterly* for 1873, p. 638 gives the best argument for a bodily resurrection, predicated upon "the first fruits," that we have ever met. It is this: "If the resurrection of Christ bears the same relation to the masses as does the first sheaf to the harvest, the work is sure; for the first sheaf could not be gathered till the harvest had reached a point *that placed the whole beyond accident.* The harvest was as certain as 'the first fruits of them that slept.'" This is slightly reasoning in a circle; proving the resurrection of all bodies by the certainty of the harvest after the first sheaf, and then proving the certainty of the harvest by the certainty of the "first fruits of them that slept." But as it is the best that can be done with the text we do not complain. The italics are the author's, indicating the strong point of his argument. Then, alas for the masses! The argument may be conclusive to those who never saw a harvest gathered, and it must be, for this is the usual way of arguing from "the first fruits," whereas, there is not a farmer's boy fifteen years of age who does not know that often after gathering "the first sheaf" most of the entire harvest is lost by some of the many foes from which it is never safe until securely housed.

If the resurrection of the bodies of men can be proven by nothing better than this (and it is an argument with which its advocates usually begin and end), then nothing is more contingent and uncertain. A farmer would laugh at a city philosopher who, passing as "the first sheaf" was gathered, would stop to assure him that "the whole is now beyond accident."

But there is not an instance in the Old Testament, or in the New, in which "the first fruits" is used in the sense of an earnest, or pledge, or pattern. If the whole harvest were to be given to the priests, then the "first sheaf" might be considered an earnest. As a gift from God to man, if there were a pledge, either by revelation or by experience, that "the whole harvest should be considered beyond accident" whenever "the first sheaf" was gathered, then "the first fruits" might be an earnest or a pattern, or both; but there is no such revelation, and there is no such experience.

Christian system, for if the dead live not, then Christ lives not, hence "your faith is vain, and ye are yet in your sins," for there is no forgiveness of sins except through Christ, to give "assurance" of whose power to forgive sins God raised Him from the dead.

He proceeds, then, to affirm that if this doctrine be eliminated from the system, there is nothing left worth embracing. In his daily conflicts, which were such that he might be said to die daily, nothing could sustain him but the hope of living hereafter. Better eat, drink, and be merry, the few days of life, than to endure such conflicts, if the dead rise not.

The second part of this chapter is devoted to an effort to disabuse the minds of the Corinthian church on the mode of that immortality. Some, at least, had assumed that the present body would be, in some way, connected with the future life, and asked, "with what body do they come?" Doubtless they were pressing the materialistic view of the subject, with the logical results of their creed, as the Sadducees had done; and, failing of a satisfactory answer, they had, like the Sadducees, come to deny the resurrection, the *anastasis*, or immortality, altogether. The question is identical in essence with that brought to Christ, and the answer proceeds on the same hypothesis, that their error is the legitimate result of their misapprehending the nature of the future life; albeit, Paul is not quite as polite as Jesus was in his method of introducing his argument. He calls the man a fool who expects to apply the laws of matter to spirit life.

As the substratum of his answer, he assures them that flesh and blood can not inherit the kingdom of God, neither can corruption inherit incorruption; hence the folly of their attempting to reason upon it from the laws of matter.

Here we sow wheat, and we reap wheat; we sow barley, and reap barley. God giveth to every seed its own body, resembling in every attribute the seed which has been sown. The same law, he says, governs animal life. Birds produce birds, and fish produce fish, and beasts produce beasts. There are different kinds of bodies, but fish never produce birds, nor wheat barley. There is also, he says, a difference between earthly bodies and heavenly bodies, they being as unlike as birds are unlike fish or beasts. The glory of the terrestrial is one, and the glory of the celestial is another, and sowing the terrestrial can no more produce a celestial than the sowing of wheat can produce any other kind of grain. We sow, for instance, a natural body, but we do not reap a natural body, for the celestial body is spiritual. We sow corruption, but our heavenly body is incorruptible.*

We can not conceive how the apostle could have proceeded more determinately to disconnect the future life from the physical of this life. He not only states that flesh and blood can not inherit the kingdom of God, but in a half dozen contrasts he shows the utter impossibility of obtaining a material existence in another world. This body is corruptible, dishonored, weak, natural, earthly; while the resurrection body is incorruptible, glorious, powerful, spiritual, heavenly.

* The phrase, "There *are* celestial bodies," should forever silence the argument which assumes that a body must be material, or at least that the spiritual body of the future life must be manufactured from the material once composing the earthly body. Angels have bodies—spiritual bodies. At least Paul says so, when he says there *are* celestial bodies. If angels can have bodies without matter, why may not man?

As if fearing that even this clear statement was not sufficient, he returns, as it were, and restates the case thus: Our present bodies are made of the earth, and they are therefore earthy; for the first man, Adam, was of the earth, earthy, and such are they also that are earthy, that is, such are his offspring; but the last Adam was the Lord from heaven, and as *is* the heavenly, such *are* they also that *are* heavenly—not such *will those be* who *shall be* heavenly.

And yet again, as though he would reiterate the argument until there could be no clinging to the earthy, he repeats: "*And as we have borne the image of the earthy we shall also bear the image of the heavenly.*" The form of every verb in these sentences should fix the time of this resurrection. "As *is* the heavenly." If Christ went up with a physical body, which was transformed into a spiritual body, so also *are* they that *are* heavenly. Our friends in heaven *are now like Christ*—as Christ *is*. But we know that our friends have not taken their physical bodies to heaven. We who are yet alive *shall bear the image of the heavenly* when, like the dying thief, we shall be with him in paradise, though our bodies moulder in the dust.

Great stress is laid upon the declaration, "It is sown a natural body, it is raised a spiritual body," and then we are told, by the believers in physical resurrection, that it is the body which is sown that is raised; the identical body which dies lives again. We interpose as a sufficient answer to this Paul's own positive declaration, "Thou sowest not that body that shall be." The figure is the same, and the language is much more emphatic. Here we leave this argument utterly demolished by the direct language of

Paul; and surely Paul would not contradict himself in so short a time.

The effort to press this beautiful statement of the mode of man's immortality into service to prove that this body shall be "reinfused" by the soul at some future time, called the resurrection, has given rise to many most contradictory interpretations of the Scriptures, each warring against the other, and neither satisfying its own friends.

With these theories we have nothing to do, further than to say that they all dishonor God in trying to devise some easy way for doing what they assume he has promised to do. If God has anywhere said that he attaches such importance to the matter which may at any time have composed our bodies, or such as compose them at the hour of death, that he watches it with special care, so that that identical matter shall be united with the soul, after interminable ages, it is the part of Christian faith to accept this promise without attempting to account for the manner in which it is to be done. The difficulties in the case are not to be wrestled with for a moment by us. Hence, to assume that there is a germ in man corresponding with the germ in the grain is utterly absurd and indefensible. If there is any promise of a future material body, it is to be *raised*, not *vegetated*. The old Jewish *Luz*, or indestructible bone, is as reasonable as such a theory. Away with all human devices to assist God in doing what to man seems difficult! Paul attempted nothing of the kind in this chapter or elsewhere: but he so states the case that, but for a most persistent purpose to maintain an indefensible proposition, he never would have been quoted as authority for a material, fleshly resurrection at the end of the world, or at any time.

CHAPTER XI.

THE SECOND COMING OF CHRIST.

WHY any other rule of interpretation should be applied to that class of scriptures which refers to the second coming of Christ than that admitted to be legitimate with others, it is impossible to conjecture. If we attempt to harmonize the views of the apostles, one of whom says that justification is of works and the other of faith, we do not become partisans of this or that, but show by the context that both agree with the doctrine of justification as elsewhere taught.

We know that, notwithstanding the decree of the council to the contrary, at least those Christians who remained at Jerusalem never ceased to offer the accustomed sacrifices of Jewish worship until after the destruction of the temple. They circumcised their children and observed the fasts and feasts of the Jews as religiously as the most devout Jew—indeed, they were themselves the most devout of their people, super-adding their Christian faith to the faith of the fathers, never dreaming that Christianity was to become a distinct and antagonistic organization. Among these was no less a disciple than the apostle James himself. Do we, therefore, quote their opinions and practices as authority for opinions and practices to-day, in reference to temple service, circumcision and ceremonial sacrifice? Certainly not;

yet the opinions which they entertained concerning the personal return of the Saviour to set up a temporal reign are quoted as authority for his yet coming, although we know that whatever they wrote or said on this subject implied an immediate appearance. Now, why should we not insist on temple worship, and daily sacrifices, and Jewish fasts and feasts, as earnestly as some do on the second advent of Christ, and enforce it as they do this, by an appeal to the views and customs of the early church?*

We know that in opinions and practices the apostles differed during their whole lives among themselves, and that the best of them changed their views on the incidentals of Christianity as they grew older and found their earlier expectations mistaken, although there is no indication in their own writings or in cotemporaneous history that they ever modified the *doctrines* of the Gospel, which they were commissioned to preach. As they began, so they ended; as they preached in Judea, so they preached in Greece and Rome. "Redemption through his blood, the forgiveness of sins."

Peter yielded his national prejudices so reluctantly that, notwithstanding the peculiar circumstances under which he was introduced to the broader mission of the Gospel by the vision of the sheet let down from heaven, and the conversion of Gentiles at the house of Cornelius, he soon afterward refused to eat with Gentile converts,

*"The first Christians had no thought of a history. They believed in an immediate return of Jesus Christ to restore all things. They supposed that the end of the world was at hand, and that the last days foretold by Joel had begun to dawn. Thus they awaited those days of refreshing from the presence of the Lord which were to inaugurate the second coming of Christ." (De Pressensé, Apostolic Age, page 48.)

and received a sharp rebuke from Paul for his back-sliding; while Paul, though a Hebrew of the Hebrews, entered at once fully into the universality of the atonement, knowing neither Greek nor Jew, bond nor free. No one insists that Peter's earlier views on the subject should be accepted instead of his later. Though these views were entertained long after that promised enduement of the Holy Ghost, which some suppose was to give clear and correct views of Christ and his mission, we easily dispose of them by the sensible concession that inspiration did not instantaneously correct the notions and prejudices of early education.

Every Sunday-school scholar knows that the disciples followed Christ to the last under the common impression of the Hebrew people, that the Messiah was to be a temporal prince, and that they were to be honored officers in the new government he was about to establish. Nothing is truer than that their sorrow at his death was intensified by their disappointment in this matter. "We had hoped that he would have redeemed Israel," was the sorrowful plaint which the two made to the stranger who inquired the cause of their sadness.

Whatever may have been the intent of the heavenly messengers who consoled the wondering disciples as they gazed into heaven on the Mount of Ascension, their language only revived the hope the disciples had so long entertained, and led them to believe that at any moment he might be expected with the pomp and power that would insure his success. Is it strange, therefore, that in their sermons they referred to the "promise of God unto the fathers," and "the hope of Israel"? The persecutions they suffered from a foreign governor only made them the more anxious for a deliverer who should rule in righteousness. Hence, in their letters, as well as in their sermons, there is frequent reference to this hope, especially in those which were written before the destruction of their national hope, in the destruction of their national capital, while such reference wholly disappears in the later writings of Paul, and in the Epistles and in the Gospel of John, which were written subsequent to that event.

On more than one occasion the Saviour himself had contributed to the formation of a hope that he would soon return with great pomp, and sit upon the throne of David. His language does not necessarily teach that. Indeed, interpreted as we can now interpret it, by the light of the events which have intervened between that teaching and our day, we know that it means something else. Yet, with the views which his disciples entertained, they could hardly see any other signification in it.

The most circumstantial account of such a promise is given by three of the evangelists, Matthew, Mark and Luke, with unimportant differences of detail, as having occurred on the Mount of Olives over against the temple. The company had just retired from that costly structure where the disciples had pointed out to him its beauty, adorned with goodly stones and gifts; to which he had replied that the time was near when not one stone should be left upon another. What conversation took place as they journeyed to the Mount is not recorded, but it was evidently about the strange declaration made concerning the future fate of Jerusalem and the temple, in which, no doubt, he had said that, in connection with that event, he would come and take vengeance upon his enemies. Hence, when Peter, and James, and John, and Andrew were seated with him, in a kind of confidential way they asked when these things should be, and what would be the sign of his coming and the end of the world.

Here are three questions in one, yet but one question. Those who have a theory to maintain assume that in the minds of the disciples the coming of Christ and the end of the world were to be synchronous, and the destruction of the temple another event; hence they arbitrarily divide the triple question into two, whereas it is certain that all were associated together as composing one grand transaction.

The answer of the Saviour, as recorded by the three evangelists, is worthy of study, especially if we would arrive at the true import of this wonderful prediction. It was to be nearly forty years before these things should take place, and there was not at that time even a remote indication of their probability.

It is contrary to all orthodox theories of the character of Christ to suppose that the declaration that he knew nothing about the time is to be taken in its literal signification. What is meant by it is not material to this discussion. He, however, gave such hints concerning the events themselves that men could not fail to recognize the sign of his coming and the end of the world when they should take place. There is a childlike simplicity in the interest which these confiding Galileans took in the alarming picture of tribulation which should be connected with that great calamity—the destruction of the temple—and we can almost see them draw near and, with bated breath, say, "Where, Lord?"

But, after all, how little they comprehended the important truths which were uttered! Their minds were occupied with that picture of their own promotion and honor which was ever uppermost in all their hopes and plans of the future. Like men from some mountain top of vision looking far away to some mountain top of beauty, they saw none of the intervening sorrows and conflicts which lay between. What could they know of the second coming of Christ, in the technical sense in which it is now used? The idea that he should go and return could by no means have entered into their minds; neither had they the remotest conception of what was to be implied in preaching the gospel throughout all the world. Their question could not possibly have included any allusion to the second coming of Christ as a part of a closing up of earth's history. That it should refer to the destruction of the temple and its accompanying incidents would be natural and probable.

After giving, quite in detail, the persecutions, and wars, and earthquakes, and famines, and pestilences which should precede the event about which they had been talking—the destruction of the temple and the city—he describes the consummation of the tribulation in one of the grandest pieces of poetic prophecy contained in the Book of God:

"Immediately after the tribulation of those days shall the sun be darkened, and the moon shall not give her light, and the stars shall fall from heaven, and the powers of the heavens shall be shaken, and upon the earth there shall be distress of nations, with perplexity, the sea and the waves roaring, men's hearts failing them for fear and for looking after those things which are coming upon the earth. And then shall appear the sign of the Son of Man in heaven, and then shall all the tribes of the earth mourn, and they shall see the Son of Man coming in the clouds of heaven with power and great glory, and he shall send his angels with a great sound of a trumpet and they shall gather together the elect from the four winds, from one end of the heaven to the other. And when these things begin to come to pass, then look up and lift up your heads, for your redemption draweth nigh." [*Strong's Harmony.*]

No historic fact is better established than that the disciples themselves and the Christians of that generation received these predictions as referring to Jerusalem and the temple. Every Christian expositor and the most reliable Jewish historians agree that when, under Titus, about thirty-six years afterwards, the city was invested and there were times of tribulation, "distress of nations and perplexity," the Christians who were in Jerusalem, warned by this prophecy, availed themselves of a temporary withdrawal of the investing army and escaped, as here admonished, and perished not in the general overthrow.

The thoughtful Bible scholar will not fail to notice the similarity of imagery existing in this and the language of Paul in his letters to the Thessalonians, written some twenty odd years later, and yet some fifteen or sixteen years before their fulfillment. With his ardent Jewish patriotism, and partaking, in common with his brethren, of the "hope of the fathers," he could not avoid entertaining the opinion that "this same Jesus would in like manner return" and fulfill "the promise to the fathers," confirmed by his own repeated promises as they understood them.

Hence, after twenty years' experience in the spiritual benefits of Christ's passion and the corroborating influences of the Holy Ghost, he still clings to a temporal Messiahship, which should at no great distance of time be ushered in with the sublime accompaniments which the Lord himself had portrayed, and which had been handed over to Paul by those who heard Him: "For the Lord himself shall descend from heaven with a shout, with the voice of the archangel, and with the trump of God. . . . The Lord Jesus shall be revealed from heaven, with his mighty angels, in flaming fire, taking vengeance on them that know not God and that obey not the Gospel of our Lord Jesus Christ."

Peter uses, substantially, the same form of speech in the third chapter of his second Epistle when referring to the same promise of the Saviour: "The day of the Lord will come as a thief in the night; in which the heavens shall pass away with a great noise, and the elements shall melt with fervent heat, and the earth also and the works that are therein shall be burned up. . . . Looking for and hasting unto the day of God wherein the heavens, being on fire, shall be dissolved and the elements shall melt with fervent heat." But all this means nothing if it does not refer to an event close at hand. Peter so understood it himself, and so it was recorded: "Wherefore, beloved, seeing that you look for such things, be diligent that you may be found of him in peace."

Is it consistent with the common notions of inspiration that the ultimate destruction of the earth and the heavens should be revealed, and that it should be revealed as being near at hand when it was thousands of years off? The event here looked for did occur in less than five years from this writing, and in the manner described according to the poetic style of such descriptions.

This high-wrought style of prophetic writing was familiar to the Jews. Isaiah had used it when describing a similar event, eight hundred years before: "Howl ye, for the day of the Lord is at hand. It shall come as a destruction from the Almighty. . . . Behold *the day of the Lord* cometh, cruel, both with wrath and fierce anger, to lay the land desolate. . . . For the stars of heaven and the constellations thereof shall not give their light. The sun shall be darkened in his going forth, and the moon shall not cause her light to shine. And I will punish the world for their evil and the wicked for their iniquity. . . . I will shake the heavens and the earth shall remove out of her place in *the wrath of the Lord of hosts,* and in *the day of his fierce anger.*" Isaiah, xiii., 6, 13.

Every idea that is contained in Paul and in Peter and in Christ's discourse is contained in this prophecy of Isaiah. He speaks of the day of the Lord—that means, of course, it is claimed, the Day of Judgment. If it does in Peter it does in Isaiah, for the form of speech is identical. With Isaiah as with Peter it was at hand, close by. It was to "lay the land desolate," and "remove the earth out of her place." He does not say by fire, but it matters not; it was to be destroyed. The heavens were to be shaken in Isaiah; they were to be dissolved in Peter, and to pass away with a great noise. The stars of heaven and the sun and moon were to be darkened with Isaiah. In Christ's prediction the sun was to be darkened and the moon turned to blood.

Why should there be an effort to apply these New Testament prophecies to something even yet future and not that of Isaiah also? The style is identical and they refer to similar events. One was fulfilled in the overthrow of Babylon, the other in the destruction of Jerusalem. Isaiah fixes the application of his prediction by saying, "And Babylon, the glory of kingdoms, shall be as when God overthrew Sodom and Gomorrah." Christ fixes the application of his prediction in a like definite manner. After predicting wars and rumors of wars, and persecution, and the abomination of desolation, and false Christs, the sun and moon darkened, the stars falling from heaven, the sign of the Son of Man in heaven, the Son of Man coming in clouds, the sound of a trumpet, the gospel preached in all the world, the gathering together of the elect from one end of the heaven to the other—after all of these which are so often claimed as belonging to that period called the end of the world, Christ says, "*This generation shall not pass till* ALL THESE THINGS be fulfilled." Let Christ be his own expositor! We repeat that all these things were fulfilled during that generation—Paul's and Peter's, as well as Christ's predictions; for they all referred to the same events.

It will not do to say that Christ spoke of the "end of the world," for every scholar knows that that phrase had a local or provincial meaning which limited it to the Roman empire or the end of that age, as we shall show hereafter. Besides, what notion could those ambitious followers of the Saviour have of such an event as the burning up of the world, just at the time in which they hoped to realize the fruition of all their ambitious purposes? The end of the world, in the sense of dogmatic theology, would have been the knell of their most cherished plans. No son of David, sitting on the restored throne of David, with themselves his chief officers, would have inspired their hopes if they thought that the world was to end just at that time.

Suppose it to be true, as it certainly is, that until after the destruction of Jerusalem the disciples accepted the promise of the Saviour as so personal that they each expected to share in the honors of that temporal kingdom which he should set up on his promised return; and suppose it to be true, as it certainly is, that their faith in their personal interest in this event was such that they had so literally construed the many promises of the Saviour that they believed that if one or more of them should die before its fulfillment they would be raised from their graves in order to participate in this grand consummation of their hopes; all this does not prove that their hopes were well-founded any more than the unanimity of their faith in their personal promotion to places of honor, in the kingdom which they supposed Christ would establish, proved them correct in regard to that hope.*

The Epistles to the Thessalonians were written about sixteen years before the invasion of Titus, and while this daily expectation of the promise of the Saviour was yet common among all Christians. But Paul lived to entertain quite

---

* "The destruction of Jerusalem was to enlarge the views of the Christians as to the future of the Church, and to give infinite expansion to the horizon of prophecy. They had now been living in daily expectation of the end of the world, and the immediate return of Christ." (De Pressensé, *Apostolic Age*, page 407.)

"The expectation of his immediate return in glory was then general. They thought that at any moment He might appear in the clouds, to judge the world." (*Ibid*, page 217.)

another view of the matter, as we shall see, while none of the apostles who wrote subsequent to the destruction of Jerusalem make any reference to the second coming of Christ, in the sense referred to by Paul in these epistles.*

John's gospel was written twenty years after the destruction of Jerusalem, and is among the latest of the several letters and essays which were gathered together long afterward to constitute the New Testament. Whatever may have been the immediate occasion of its production, it is not probable that he would have wholly omitted to mention so important a speech of the Saviour if, in his mind, any part of it yet referred to a future event so absorbing in its nature as the second coming of Christ to judge the world must have appeared to him. He was one of the four to whom it was delivered, and he shared, with his brother disciples, the awe which its fearful predictions inspired. But now more than a half century had passed since he sat with that company, "over against the temple." Its fearful revolutions and bitter persecutions had not only swept away the companions of his earlier life, but Jerusalem was a desolation, and, true to the prediction of the Saviour, and to the visions granted to himself on the isle of Patmos, the beautiful temple had perished amidst those terrible con-

* "The views of the apostle as to the nearness of the closing period of history seem to have undergone some modifications. In the first stage of his career, he supposes that but a very few years will intervene before the coming of the day of the Lord. He is even persuaded that it will arrive before his own death. Subsequently, in the Roman prison, on the eve of sealing his testimony with his blood, he receives new light. This is very evident from his epistle to the Philippians, 'For I am in a strait betwixt two, having a desire to depart *and be with Christ*, which is far better.'" (De Pressensé, *Apostolic Age*, page 286.)

vulsions which were but feebly portrayed in the language of Christ, and in John's own visions of wrathful vials, and the white and the red horses and their riders, and the angel with one foot on sea and the other on the land swearing that time should be no longer.

In these fifty years he had learned that there was a higher honor awaiting the sons of Zebedee than that sought for them by their ambitious mother, to sit one on the right hand and the other on the left, in the kingdom which she and they expected would soon be set up. While there is no allusion whatever in his Gospel to the prediction so minutely described by others, there is in the Epistles a reference to the appearance of the Saviour, and what we shall then be —not mere attendants, but like him, for we shall see him as he is;—not as he will be, or as he was, or even as we think him to be, but as he IS!

No doubt, at the time of writing his Epistles to the Thessalonians Paul did expect, in common with the Christians of his times, that Christ was about to fulfill the promise made by the angels at the time of the ascension, and in the manner which their ambitious imaginings had prescribed; but we have seen that he and they were mistaken in the purport of the words of Christ, although, a few years after the death of this apostle, Christ did come and fulfill his promise; and he fulfilled their expectations as literally as he carried out the poetic portions of the prediction, and as literally as was fulfilled the prophecy of the sounding of a trumpet and the darkening of the heavens, and the falling of the stars. And all these were as literally fulfilled in the destruction of Jerusalem as the corresponding poetic figures of Isaiah were fulfilled in the destruction of Babylon. Yet there are not wanting those who argue that because the literal stars did not fall at the destruction of Jerusalem therefore the prediction must yet be unfulfilled, and it must therefore relate to the end of the world! They do not argue that because in the overthrow of Babylon the stars of heaven and the constellations thereof were to cease to give light, and the world and the wicked were to be punished, and it was not done, therefore the prophecy was not fulfilled.

After all, how strangely some men sink all their common sense and their education in maintaining some of their theological notions! To an age which regarded the stars as mere atoms, not any larger than hail stones, and mere attendants upon the earth, it was possible to conceive of such a thing as the falling of stars as a literal fact; but since science has demonstrated that the smallest fixed star is millions of times larger than our earth, the idea of their all falling to the earth is too absurd to command respectable contempt; yet there are educated men who look for this very thing, and as firmly believe it will come as they believe anything spoken of in the Bible.

Expositors lose our respect when they say, speaking of this prediction: Here its application to Jerusalem ends, and there its application to the end of the world begins;—that was fulfilled in the destruction of Jerusalem, but this relates to the end of the world, the day of the Lord; and we are inclined to believe that they do not much respect themselves; certainly they do not respect each other, for no two fix the dividing line at the same place.

Suppose that we do eliminate from the teachings of Paul, and Peter, and James, so much as was evidently tinged by their Jewish prejudices and national hopes, and suppose that we regard as merely uninspired *opinions* those passages which imply a re-appearance of the dead (but not the bodies of the dead) at the time of his coming, we do no more than Second Adventists do when they eliminate apostolic opinions as to the nearness of that coming. We believe the apostles were right as to the nearness of his coming, but wrong as to some of their notions of the details of that coming. Second Adventists believe they were wrong as to the time of his coming, but so eminently correct as to the details of his coming that they are prepared to anathematize those who dare to question the correctness of those opinions. Neither do we worse than every American patriot does when he eliminates Paul's notion of the sin of rebellion, or some of his notions on slavery, or his rules for greeting one another with a holy kiss, not to mention many other things which were evidently the utterances of his peculiar surroundings.

We have already alluded to the universal concessions of scholars that the words rendered *end of the world* should be rendered *end of the age*, or end of the present order of things. The language of Christ, at the temple, must have been a surprise to those disciples who had with so much satisfaction pointed out the beauty and costliness of that building, when he announced that the time was near at hand when not one stone should be left upon another. No wonder, therefore, that they sought an early opportunity for an explanation, in the triple-single question we have already quoted.

Having never dreamed that the death of

Christ would be any different from the death of any other great personage, and feeling sure that even that would be delayed until he should have set up the kingdom of great David's greater Son, how could they attach to the coming of Christ any such notion as that now attached to it by Second Adventists? Groaning under the yoke of a foreign oppressor, from which, in their imaginations, they were to be delivered by the inauguration of this new king; and believing that each of them would occupy an important place under the new government; and inferring from what had been said that the national calamity would be somehow connected with the overthrow of this oppressor; it was exactly in the spirit of the impatient Psalmist who, when similarly situated, exclaimed: "Lord, how long shall the wicked triumph?" that they asked, "What shall be the sign of thy coming and of the end of the present system of oppression and wrong—of the present order of things?"

Any other construction of this question is forced and unnatural; for they were certainly not looking for a destruction of the earth, and a winding up of all temporalities just at the moment that they should at once realize the hope of Israel, and attain to the acme of their personal ambitions.

The Saviour evidently so understood them, and he answers accordingly, though he predicts coming events of a very different character from what they had anticipated. He portrays a degree of tribulation such as earth had never seen, and then adds that his gospel should first be preached in all the world—*in all the inhabited parts of the world*, as the original word always means. It is a different word from that just used by the disciples, and erroneously translated *world.* The two are never used interchangeably in good Greek. Mark's recollection of the word used was "among all *nations.*"

That the Gospel was so preached even before Paul's death we have Paul's testimony. In Col. i., 23, he says: "The Gospel was preached to every creature under the whole heaven," showing that, according to the views of the apostles themselves, at least that much of the preliminary events of that wonderful prediction had taken place, preparatory to the great event which was to follow. No wonder, therefore, that they constantly looked for the Saviour, and said evermore, "The coming of the Lord draweth nigh."

We admit that the most literal meaning of the language of the *two men** who accosted the wondering disciples on Mount Olivet implies a personal return of the Saviour in a form visible to them: "This same Jesus, which is taken up from you into heaven, shall so come in like manner as ye have seen him go into heaven." (Acts i., 11.)

Then he must be visible to them only, for this Jesus, since his death, had been seen only by his disciples, and by them only on chosen occasions. Yet such a return leaves out all of the usual fillings of the picture which tradition has thrown

*"May they not have been the *two men* who were with Christ on the Mount of Transfiguration, Moses and Elias?" (*Whedon's Notes on Acts.*)

We answer, Yes, or any other two men. David and Samuel, Daniel and Isaiah, or Moses and Joshua. It is just what *we* should expect of any of the good men who had lived and died, and who still live, as Christ teaches that Abraham and Isaac and Jacob do. *Two men* is the exact meaning of the sacred writers. The time will come, and not far hence, when Scripture expositors will not find it necessary to substitute angels for men in such Scriptures. They were *men,* not ghosts nor angels, just *men,* nothing more or less.

around that event, so insufficiently authorized by the Scriptures. Here we have no trumpet, no burning worlds, no falling stars, no legions of angels, no setting of thrones, no judgment. The *manner* of this event is sublime in its simplicity and silence, and he was to come *in like manner*.

If this text refers at all to a personal return of the Saviour it is absolutely fatal to the popular theory. If it proves anything, it proves too much for those who introduce it as a witness. No one passage is more directly oppósed to the popular notions of that event. That noiseless ascension, that friendly cloud, cannot be transformed into the *manner* which it is assumed will attend the opening of graves and the burning of worlds.

But is anything more taught by this than is intended by Christ's own words: "I will come and receive you to myself"? (John xiv., 3). Is it not the same thing? If not, why not? Yet it would be such an outrage upon the evident meaning of Christ to wrest this text from its surroundings, and make it tributary to the doctrine of Second Adventists, that Dr. Adam Clarke, himself a Second Adventist, says it means: "I will come again after my resurrection, and give you the fullest assurance of this state of blessedness, and confirm you in the faith by my grace and the effusion of my spirit."

But if all this did not remove the passage from the list of proof texts, and even if it were tenfold more positive in its language, still it would not be admissible to prove the second coming of Christ by it alone, in opposition to the otherwise uniform teachings of inspiration. That method of interpretation is no longer tolerated in good society. It might have answered a hundred years ago, when it was customary to comfort the elect by learned discourses from the Scripture: "Jacob have I loved and Esau have I hated," to prove the doctrine of unconditional personal election and reprobation. We hear no more of that among scholars—it is hardly heard any longer even on the outskirts of civilization, among the fast disappearing "hardshells" of the past generation.

Dr. Adam Clarke, who believed with the best of modern Biblical scholars that the book of Revelation was written before the destruction of Jerusalem, thus disposes of three favorite proof texts of this dogma: "'Behold he cometh with clouds' (Rev. i., 7); this relates perhaps to his coming to destroy Jerusalem. 'Behold, I come quickly' (Rev. xxii., 12); I come to establish my cause, comfort and support my followers, and punish the wicked. 'Surely, I come quickly' (Rev. xxii., 20); this may be truly said to every person in every age."

We repeat that the phrases: "the end," "end of the world," "last day," "day of the Lord," and kindred phrases nowhere occur in the Bible referring to the closing up of earthly affairs. They cannot be so applied without doing violence to the opinions of eminent commentators, both ancient and modern, who are entitled to a respectful consideration. Dr. Strong, in his *Notes on the Gospels*, p. 287, says: "The question, 'What shall be the sign of thy coming and the end of the world?' is deeply imbued with the prevailing expectations of the Jews that the national operations of the Messiah would occasion such political convulsions as might indeed endanger for the time their present institutions, but would result in their re-establishment, with fresh glory and universal authority."

Richard Watson, in his *Exposition*, p. 247, says: "Here the disciples appear to employ the phrase, *end of the world*, for that glorious manifestation of their master which they anticipated; one of honor and glory to them, and destruction to his enemies."

Dr. Joseph Benson, in his notes on Matt. xxiv., 3, says: "The disciples inquire concerning two things: first, the time of the destruction of Jerusalem; second, the sign of it."

Dr. Adam Clarke, on Matt. xvi., 28, says: "Very clearly the whole passage speaks of the destruction of the Jewish polity." On Matt. xxiv., 3, he says: "*End of the world* means end of the age, the end of the Jewish economy."

But we have a still more ancient commentator of some repute, and whose expositions of Scripture are worthy of consideration, and his name is Paul. Speaking of Christ, he says: "But now *in the end of the world* hath he appeared" (Heb. ix., 26). This, at least, shows Paul's opinion of the end of the world. Again: "In these *last days* hath spoken to us by his Son (Heb. i., 2).

We have still another ancient commentator, and his name is Peter. Standing up before his brethren, he commented on the words of Joel, and said: "This is that which was spoken by Joel to come to pass *in the last days*."

We have still another. Christ himself becomes his own expositor. He says: "The harvest is *the end of the world*." Then, as fixing the time of the harvest, he says: "Lift up your eyes, for the fields are white *already to the harvest!*"

Are we wrong, therefore, in saying that these phrases never occur as referring to the winding up of earth's history? Explained by Christ himself, and by Paul and Peter, and by eminent scholars of modern times, they have another meaning. In the face of such authority is it not almost impious to claim their use in the sense which implies a destruction of the earth and earthly things?

But does not the phrase, "The day of the Lord," mean the Day of Judgment? It certainly does in Peter and similar Scriptures if it does in Isaiah, where it is twice used, and where Isaiah himself applies it to the destruction of Babylon. The form of speech is the same in Peter, and the style of Peter's prediction is identical with that of Isaiah, and the events refered to are as similar as events nine hundred years apart could be. Will any one tell why it must be made to mean a future general judgment in Peter, and be restricted to the judgment of Babylon in Isaiah?

But a greater than Isaiah or Peter throws light upon it. Christ himself tells us what his day means. "Abraham rejoiced to see *my day*. He saw *it*, and was glad" (John viii., 56). This cannot, by any stretch of imagination, be made to refer to a remote and ever-receding day of judgment, in the sense in which it is used in modern pulpits.

With the utmost deference, therefore, to the learned men who have sought to maintain an unscriptural theory as to the mode of our future life, by applying the language of Christ in direct opposition to his own words, we conclude that not a word of his prediction can be pressed into service to prove his second coming in the technical sense which dogmatic theology assumes. Even though all that the apostles wrote concerning the coming of Christ had reference to the end of time, we should yet be compelled to find an apology for them. Their language means nothing if it does not mean that the event of which they wrote was near at hand. But nearly two thousand years have passed, and the end is not yet; on the contrary, this earth seems to be in the very spring-time of a vigorous youth. Its railroads, and telegraphs, and steamships, and printing-presses do not indicate the sere and yellow leaf of decay, but the preparations for a new life for which all past ages were preliminary and preparatory. If Paul was talking of an early closing up of terrestrial affairs, he was as badly mistaken as when he enjoined silence upon women. The world refuses to wind up, and women make excellent preachers, in spite of him.

Finally, why should we be shut up to apostolic notions of the end of time, even assuming that they meant to teach the doctrine of a second coming, still future, with the usual supposed concomitants of such an event, and yet reject their opinions concerning the beginning? It is not probable that they knew any more of the future of earth than of the past any more of the method of its ending than of the manner of its creation, or of its shape and size. They knew that through Jesus they were authorized to preach repentance and the forgiveness of sins, but beyond that they were quite as likely to be mistaken as other men, on questions and opinions which were but remotely, if at all, germain to the specialty of their mission.

But there is manifestly a using of the words

which relate to a coming of Christ in a sense which does not refer to the overthrow of Jerusalem, nor yet to the Day of Judgment. There is a personal application of this form of speech which has not escaped even the most ardent of Second Adventists. They cannot preach, or write, or lecture on the subject without rising higher than their creed, and being wiser than their theory. They uniformly close their wild speculations by a word of sound sense, and say: "Whatever may be the manner, and whenever the time, Christ comes practically to each of us whenever he comes to call us hence by his messenger, death." *

This is Scriptural as well as sensible; and it has the sanction of the Saviour. His parables abound with such exhortations as these: "Watch, therefore, for ye know not at what hour your Lord doth come." "Be ye also ready, for in such an hour as ye think not, the Son of Man cometh." "Watch, therefore, for ye know not when the Master of the House cometh." These admonitions are connected with such parables as the foolish virgins, the householder, and the faithful servants.

Even in the discourse which referred to the destruction of Jerusalem it would be meaningless in any other sense, for not many, if any, of those who heard him could live to see the event spoken of. Is it not strange, therefore, that by Second Adventists, in every case where refer-

* "The individual death is the virtual coming of the Son of Man."—*Whedon's Notes, Vol. I., p.* 291.

"The majestic coming of Christ is going on constantly in the process of history."—*Lange on Matt., p.* 431.

"Jesus may be said to come quickly to every person in every age." *Dr. A. Clarke, Rev. xxii.,* 22.

ence to the coming of Christ occurs in the writings of the apostles, it is claimed as a proof of a second personal coming and the supposed end of the world, while the application which Christ himself gives is dragged in grudgingly, as an afterthought or exhortation?

It will help us to understand the frequent allusion to the coming of Christ in the sense which Christ himself certainly authorizes, to remember that death is not a separation of the soul, as a part of the man, from the body, another part of the man, for an indefinite but long period, the soul to wander a naked ghost until a general resurrection, but it is the *man* being unclothed of mortality, that he may be clothed upon with immortality.

In this light, how intelligible are the most of those passages which refer to the coming of Christ! "As in Adam all die, even so in Christ shall all be made alive." "Christ the first fruits, afterward they that are Christ's" when he comes to call them from the tribulations and duties of earth to his society in the land of spirits. They that are Christ's,—those who are watching like the wise virgins, will be made to live, as the dying thief was, at that period which is known in the language of men as death; and they shall be like Christ and be forever with him.

Even that oft-quoted language of Paul, "For our conversation [our citizenship] is in heaven; whence also we look for the Saviour, the Lord Jesus Christ, who shall change our vile bodies and fashion them like unto his glorious body," has a beauty and significance from this standpoint that is never seen from any other. Remembering that Paul and Peter speak of the body as a tabernacle for the real *man*, which may be "put off" or exchanged for a better one; as a garment of which we may be "unclothed," that we may be "clothed upon" with something better, and of another fashion, even a heavenly; and remembering that departing from this we are at once with the Lord, and like him, and remembering also that the word which is rendered "change" is often used very nearly in the sense of "exchange"—"These things have I *transferred* [exchanged] to myself and to Apollos," (1 Cor., iv., 6)—there can be no violence done to the meaning of Paul to thus paraphrase his language: "We are in fact not citizens of earth, but of heaven, whence we constantly look for the Saviour, the Lord Jesus Christ, who shall change these bodies of humiliation, which are fitted only to earth, for bodies like unto the body of glory which was seen upon the Mount of Transfiguration, and which shall be in fashion in heaven."

Such a paraphrase makes it consistent with the uniform teachings of the Bible elsewhere, especially with such Scriptures as those which represent death as the unclothing of the man, preparatory to the clothing upon with the heavenly house—the house of heavenly fashion.

The soldier returning from the battle-field to the endearments and rest of home might well soliloquise, "I am only a soldier here and a stranger. These tattered and camp-worn garments are unsuited for the society of civil life, but at the borders of my own land I shall meet my father, who shall change these vile garments and fashion them like unto the clothing which he wears, for he is abundantly able to do this, and he is as willing as he is able," and the weary soldier would tread firmer and faster as he would anticipate such a change of clothing, without dreaming that the old filthy blue would become the basis of his new outfit. When we talk of changing garments in spring or autumn, and adopting a fashion better suited to the coming season, we do not propose to make over the worn-out rags which we mean to drop when we step into the new. No more does Christ propose to make our heavenly body out of our cast-off earthly body. We know that in fact he does not do this, for it lies all decayed and offensive in the grave, and we know that the soul, *the real man*, is not a naked ghost in heaven, for the man is with the Lord and like him—"as he is"—"as the angels of God in heaven." Therefore this *change* cannot be a transformation merely.

We add that those who insist upon the most literal meaning of such words of this text as indicate a transformation of the old body into the new must take also the most literal meaning of other words, and teach that the Christian, being a citizen of heaven, owes no duties to the institutions of earth. This has been tried in a few extreme cases, but usually the believer in a literal interpretation has found himself in the hospital for the insane, as a maniac.

From this standpoint how full of meaning and consolation is that other language of Paul: "When Christ, who is our life, shall appear, then shall ye also appear with him in glory." The cold, cheerless view, that this refers to his appearing at that remote event called the Judgment, leaves the man in a state of unconsciousness or sleep, or at least in but a partially happy state, awaiting that event which is to open glory for him. But, viewed as Paul viewed it, we find the man going at once with Christ into glory, as the penitent thief did—*then*, at that very moment, not indefinite ages hence. "I AM the life," says Christ, not I *will be*.

John, in his gospel, written long after the fulfillment of Christ's prediction concerning Jerusalem, makes no mention of that coming which had become history, yet he beautifully alludes to that coming to which Christ referred when he said, "Be ye also ready, for at an hour ye think not the Son of Man cometh." "It doth not yet appear what we shall be," said he, "but we know that when he appears we shall be like him, for we shall see him as he is." Mark the beauty of this teaching. "*When* he appears"—at that very moment—"we shall be like him, for we shall see him as he is," not as he was, not as he will be, but *as he is!* The dead are with the Lord and they are *now* like him.

Such an interpretation of these references to the coming of the Saviour makes the Bible consistent with itself, and gives such a view of Heaven as the martyrs had when they triumphed in death—such as dying Christians now have. In this light death loses its sting, the grave gains no victory, for mortality is at once and forever swallowed up in life.

And we may add that there is no middle ground between such outbreaks of fanaticism as swept over the country about the year 1843, and which has a local existence more or less all the time, and the views here set forth. If the second coming of Christ is to be literal, it is equally literally the duty of every man to expect it daily. "It draweth nigh," is "at the door." So that those who "look for those things" are wiser in their generation than those who believe the absurdities as to manner and reject the absurdities as to time. Millerites and their kith are the only consistent Second Adventists.

CHAPTER XII.

VERBAL CRITICISMS—ANASTASIS, EGERSIS—THE WORD OF THE LORD—RISE FIRST.

WITH a wholesome disrelish for that style of discussion which falls behind a display of learning in an emergency, and resorts to nice distinctions in the words of the original languages of the Bible, we call attention to a few words which often occur in connection with the subject under discussion. We do it, distinctly announcing that whatever argument may be found in this examination is merely corroborative and cumulative, not vital. The argument of the book is complete without this; yet, in deference to the tastes of some, we introduce it.

We announce further, that while we consider the argument of this chapter unanswerable, we shall not be surprised if some valiant Greek should array against it even a greater display of learning, and completely overthrow it, in his judgment at least. Indeed it will be strange if this is not done, since for ages Greek has met Greek on theological subjects with as relentless a "tug of war" and with as indecisive results as of old Greek met Greek on the field of carnal strife. While it is yet unsettled whether *baptizo* means to sprinkle or to immerse, and whether the preposition *en* means *into* or *near by*, and whether *apo* means *out of* or *away from*, we shall not be dogmatic enough to pronounce all persons wilfully blind who do not agree with our conclusions from the following statements.

In the first place, the chief if not the only plausible argument against our exposition of the fifteenth chapter of first Corinthians is, that in the phrase, "It is sown a natural body, it is raised a spiritual body," the pronoun *it* must have *body* for its antecedent, and therefore the body that is sown must be the body which is raised. This is sufficiently answered by the language of Paul, "Thou sowest not that body that shall be." But it may be further answered by the fact that there is no word in the original answering to our translator's *it*. The idiom of the Greek language indeed requires the use of this unpersonal pronoun in the translation, but no good Greek scholar will insist that such a use of such a pronoun gives any authority for its use as a personal pronoun with an antecedent, any more than a similar use of the same word in the impersonal phrases, "it rains," "it is said," "it is seen," and hundreds of like character, requires it to have an antecedent.

We have already stated that many of the best Greek scholars of modern times maintain that the word *anastasis* always refers to the after life, and seldom, if ever, to the method of reaching that immortality, and that, though always rendered *resurrection*, it never refers solely to the act of rising, but includes also the idea of living afterwards, if not this wholly; while its companion word, *egersis*, is not a synonym, but refers to the act of raising or arousing, and seldom, if ever, including the idea of the after life, which is always implied in *anastasis*.*

* "*Anastasis*, the word constantly used throughout the New Testament for resurrection, signifies a rising again, a life after death, another state of the same person, but never once, that I know of, signifies or even implies a resurrection of the same body."—*Bishop Newton.*

Let us collate a few passages of Scripture in which these words occur, and we shall see that they are never used interchangeably, but that the distinction here stated is carefully observed.

Matthew (xvi., 21) and Luke (ix., 22), in giving their version of Christ's reference to his rising, use the passive form and represent him as being "raised again the third day." They each use *egeiro.* Mark, however, (viii., 31) uses the active form, as including Christ's own power, and properly uses the verb *anistemi.* "After three days shall rise again." In the account given by each of these three evangelists of another reference by Christ to the same event, we find each of the three referring to it as Christ's own act, and each uses *anistemi.* "And the third day he shall rise again."

We find the same careful use of these two words in the accounts which the evangelists give of the fact itself. We have the angels in their statement saying: "He is risen." (Matt. xxviii., 6, 7; Luke xxiv., 6; Mark xvi., 6.) Here is reference only to the disappearance of the body from the grave, hence each writer uses *egeiro.* But when the disciples come to speak of him they say *he is alive,* hence that strange disappearance means more than the removal of the body from the grave. "For as yet they knew not the Scripture, that he must rise again from the dead" (*anistemi.*)

At the meeting of the disciples in which the unexpected disappearance of the body was discussed, we have "The Lord is risen indeed"—(*egeiro*) (Luke xxiv., 34)—while in Christ's exposition of the Scripture to them, he uses the word which implies power and living, hence when he says, "It behooved Christ to rise from the dead the third day," he uses *anistemi.* (Luke xxiv., 46.)

Notice the choice of words with the two men in shining garments, which can hardly be accidental. In Luke xxiv., 6, they say "He is not here, but is risen," (*egeiro*) alluding to the disappearance of the body. But in the next verse they mean more than that, and consequently say, "Remember that he said unto you: The Son of Man must rise again," (*anistemi*) plainly teaching the after life, not the mere removal of the body from the grave. Yet when the promise was made, both Matthew (xvi., 21; xvii., 23) and Luke (ix., 22) understood him to refer only to a raising of the body, and accordingly use the verb *egeiro,* to awake, arouse, arise.

The noun *egersis* occurs but once in the whole New Testament. Its meaning there cannot be mistaken. In Matthew xxvii., 53, we have: "And came out of the graves after his resurrection" (*egersis*). There is the best of reasons for not using *anastasis* in this connection. The *anastasis* of Christ took place when the Father received his spirit and when he and the thief were, that very day, in Paradise; while the *egersis,* the rising up of the body, was delayed some thirty-six hours or more. The rising of the bodies which came out of the graves was after the *egersis,* or raising, of Christ's body. Here we have the active form of the verb, yet we have the verb *egeiro.* "Many bodies of the saints which slept arose," for the rising was not to the *anastasis*—the future life, but merely an exceptional and miraculous event for a specific purpose.

We find the distinction between these two words carefully observed in the account of the *egersis,* or raising up of Lazarus. When Christ spoke to Martha he had reference to the immortality of Lazarus, and said "Thy brother shall rise again" (*anistemi*), meaning more than the miracle which he was about to perform. Martha's answer referred to the same thing, for she had never thought of the resuscitation of his dead body at that time, hence she uses both the verbal and substantive form of *anastasis* in her answer, whereupon Christ replies, "I *am* the *resurrection* [the *anastasis*, the immortality] and the life." Subsequently, every reference which is made to the risen Lazarus is with the verb *egeiro*, although the active form of the verb is used. "Whom he raised," "whom he had raised," "and raised him from the dead." (John xii., 1, 9, 17).

The reason is obvious. There is in neither case any reference to the *anastasis*. Lazarus had to die again, as other men, and be raised to immortality, to the *anastasis*, as other men.

The same *egeiro* is used when speaking of all the dead whom he had miraculously raised: "The dead are raised up," (Matt. xi., 5, Luke vii., 22), for these miracles did not procure immortality, they only restored the subjects of them to their natural lives. The *anastasis* was to follow as with all others.

Let us look at Paul's use of these words in his celebrated argument in the fifteenth of First Corinthians, in which the doctrine of man's immortality is purposely and fully discussed. It will be seen that the words are never used interchangeably, and also that the distinction we have noticed is carefully observed. In the fourth verse we have, "He rose again the third day." *Egeiro* is here used, not *anistemi* as would be proper if he had referred to his soul-resurrection—his *anastasis*—his after-living; but, referring only to the removal of the body from the grave as an attestation of his mission, he uses *egeiro*. . . .

In the twelfth verse we have: "If Christ be preached that he rose from the dead," (*egeiro*). This is as it should be, for there is a reference simply to his *egersis*, the act or fact of rising. But when he comes to the question of immortality he says, "How say some among you that there is no *anastasis?*" no future life. If reference had been only to the fact of rising he should have used the noun *egersis* as Matthew did (xxvii., 53), when refering to that only.

In the thirteenth verse we have the same choice of words. "If there be no resurrection [no *anastasis*, no future life—no immortality] then is Christ not risen," (*egeiro*). Plainly this conclusion would follow, for he was arguing in favor of immortality through Christ, whose *egersis* or rising from the grave was proof of authority.

In the fourteenth verse, pursuing the same line of argument, and reaching the same conclusion from the same premises, we have: "If Christ be not risen" (*egeiro*) then the whole Christian system is a failure, for it is without sufficient attestation.

In verses 16, 17, 20, we have: "For if the dead rise not (*egeiro*) then is Christ not raised, (*egeiro*), and if Christ be not raised (*egeiro*) your faith is vain. But now is Christ risen from the dead," (*egeiro*). But in the twenty-first verse we have a change of words because there is a change of meaning. Coming to the subject of his discourse, human immortality, he uses *anastasis*, not *egersis* as would have been proper if he had been talking of the rising of the physical body as he had been of the body of Christ. "By man came the resurrection of the dead;"

the *anastasis*, the future living, not merely the act of coming from the grave.

Again, in the twenty-ninth and thirty-second verses we have the same *egeiro*. "If the dead rise not at all"—if they are not aroused from their slumbers—if death is the end of man. In the thirty-fifth verse we again have *egeiro* with special significance, "How are the dead raised up?" How is that change effected? How are they aroused? With what body do they come? referring to the idea of the objector that a body must be raised as Christ's body was raised. In the answer he uses the word *anastasis*, not *egersis* as he would have done had he been writing of the arousing of the same body; *and as the sacred writers always do when referring to the mere act of raising the body of Christ!* "So also is the resurrection"—the *anastasis*. In the next breath he again uses *egeiro* in reference to the *act* of raising: "It *is raised* in incorruption—*is raised* in power,—*is raised* a *spiritual* body." We have the same *egeiro* in verse fifty-second. "The dead shall be raised incorruptible," shall be aroused, waked up to a life of immortality.

Bearing in mind that there is in this chapter a distinct denial of a bodily resurrection (v. 50), "Flesh and blood"—the natural body—"can not inherit the kingdom of God," and that Paul more than once says that that which is raised is not what is sown, but something as entirely unlike it as birds are unlike fishes or wheat unlike other grain, his use of *egeiro* instead of *anistemi* is significant, seeing that he is referring all the time only to the act of arousing, or awaking; not to the living afterwards—not to the *anastasis*.

That the word *anastasis*, which is always rendered resurrection, seldom, if ever, refers to the fact of rising, we cite a few more passages to prove. In the selection of a successor to Judas it became desirable to have one who should be a witness of the resurrection of Christ, as that was implied by the word *anastasis*. Now, none of the disciples had witnessed the rising of Christ, the *egersis*. Probably not even the Roman soldiers had witnessed that, yet Matthias and the eleven had all witnessed his resurrection, his *anastasis*, during the forty days which intervened before his ascension. They had seen him living again, though not one of them had seen him rise.

That the word *egeiro*, so appropriately used everywhere to speak of the fact of rising, does not include all that is implied by *anistemi* is further evident from several examples of its use. In John v., 21, we have, "The Father raiseth up the dead and quickeneth them," referring to the gift of immortality. Here the verb is *egeiro*, but it must be accompanied by the verb which implies quickening, or giving immortal life, for it alone is not sufficient to express the transition from mortality to immortality; but *anistemi* does. In John vi., 40, 54, we have the whole idea conveyed by *anistemi*, "I will raise him up at the last day."

This difference is equally manifest in Eph. v., 14, "Awake (*egeiro*), thou that sleepest, arise from the dead (*anistemi*), and Christ shall give thee light." The arousing from the sleep of sin is one thing, the living a life of righteousness is quite another, just as awaking from death is one thing, living in the *anastasis* is another.

In Acts the words, to a careless reader, seem to be used interchangeably, but they never are.

This difference is everywhere observed. *Anistemi* always means more than *egeiro*, the latter referring to the mere fact of rising; the former to the living afterward. Thus in Acts ii., 24 and 32, we have, "Whom God hath raised up," and "This Jesus hath God raised up, . . being at the right hand of God exalted." As might be expected, here we have *anistemi*, for the resurrection is coupled with demonstrations of power. Again (iii., 26), "God, having raised up his son Jesus, sent him to bless you." Again (xvii., 3), "Alleging that Christ must needs have suffered and risen again from the dead." Again (xvii., 31), "He will judge the world in righteousness by that man whom he hath ordained, whereof he hath given assurance unto all men in that he hath raised him from the dead." Again (xxiv., 23), "That Christ should suffer and that he should be the first that should rise from the dead." In all these we have *anistemi*, and the context shows in each case that the aim was to call attention to the after life of Christ and the power consequent upon his now living, more than to the mere fact of his rising—his *egersis*. "Should. show light to the people"—"should judge the world in righteousness"—"This Jesus is the Christ"—"Sent him to bless you," are the explanatory phrases.

On the other hand, we have *egeiro* in all of the following passages, in each of which the fact of his rising is the leading thought. "Whom God hath raised from the dead" (iii., 18; iv., 10). "The God of our fathers raised up Jesus" (v., 30). "Him God raised the third day" (x., 40). "But God raised him from the dead" (xiii., 30). "Whom God raised again" (xiii., 37). "Incredible that God should raise the dead" (xxvi., 8).

The same distinction is observed in the language of Paul in that beautiful sentence in 1 Thess. iv., 16, "The dead in Christ shall rise first." If this referred to the raising of bodies from the countless graves of earth, as is usually supposed, the apostle would have used *egeiro* as the proper verb, as in the examples just given. But no; he means that the dead in Christ shall be changed from mortality to immortality, shall live *before* that day, not the first thing on that day as some suppose, and he uses the verb *anistemi* in its most obvious sense.

By not observing the proper meaning of the words used in this connection this language of Paul has been distorted from its true meaning so as to give countenance to the popular notion of the second coming of Christ. In the first place, great stress is laid upon the phrase, "By the Word of the Lord," as if Paul claimed special inspiration upon this one subject, whereas he means only that he refers to the same thing as that to which the Lord referred in his discourse as he sat over against the temple. The preposition *en* is never used in the New Testament, to our knowledge, in the sense of *by authority*, but it is often used in the sense of *according to*, or *in conformity with*, and has that meaning here. Again, the ordinary picture of the resurrection at the last day, when the trump shall sound, is that the graves shall be opened, and the first thing to be done on that day, or as it is expressed in poetry, "on the resurrection morn," will be the raising of the bodies which had been dead thousands, and probably millions of years; then, after all this is done, and not until *all* is done, we which are alive and remain shall be changed in a moment. It spoils all this picture to look at the language of Paul in the light of good Greek. The word *anistemi* is used instead of *egeiro;* and the adverb which is rendered *first* is used here in the sense of *before,* which is by far its most common meaning in the New Testament; as, "Seek *first,* [before all other things,] the kingdom, etc."

Taken in connection with the discourse of Christ, and taking the words in their most obvious sense, and remembering that it was written just before the fulfillment of the prediction which was to be all fulfilled during that generation, the passage means: "this we say on authority of the Lord's teaching; . . . and those who have died in Christ shall live in their immortality before that day of tribulation."

CHAPTER XIII.

THE ARGUMENT FROM EXPERIENCE. THE LANGUAGE OF DYING CHRISTIANS INCONSISTENT WITH A BELIEF IN A BODILY RESURRECTION. THE FAITH, BETTER THAN THE CREED.

IT is a noteworthy fact that the language of dying Christians, expressive of their hopes of immortality, is seldom, if ever, consistent with a belief in a far off future bodily resurrection, whatever views they entertained on this subject in health. We do not allege that their opinions have been changed by any process of reasoning, or that they have been changed at all. Possibly they have not been; stili the fact is of value in determining the mode of man's immortality. We cannot call to mind a single instance, ancient or modern, in the death of any Christian of whom we ever read or heard, in which any portion of the language of exultant faith, such as is not uncommon on the death-bed, referred, even remotely, to a hope of a bodily resurrection. The instincts of such an hour, if not, indeed, the inspirations, ignore all creeds, and seize the beautiful and truthful, in spite of former opinions; and Paradise, with its central personage, the blessed Redeemer, and with the loved ones of life gone on before, opens up to the realizing faith. This may be light, neither from the Scriptures nor from science, upon the darkness which hangs around the mode of man's immortality. Let us call it light from experience.

If Paul ever taught the doctrine of a bodily

resurrection, by letter or by sermon, as we are sure he never did, his dying faith denied his living creed and seized the sublimer and more comforting truths of Christ's teachings. In youth he had been ambitious of earthly fame, and had, as he supposed, much in which he might glory; but, that he might win Christ, he renounced all this, counting all things loss which he had most cherished in the line of his former purposes, and he learned to glory in the cross only. If, in his earlier ministry, he had partaken of the common mistake of the disciples, and imagined that Christ would soon appear with pomp and great power, certainly before his own death, (1 Thess. iv., 15–17), this hope, long deferred, had faded away. The twelve years which had elapsed between the writing of the letters in which this belief is so confidently expressed and the time of his last imprisonment at Rome had chastened his early ambitions, and now, no longer expecting such a display, he appropriates the best of the promises to his own use, and says with true Christian triumph—"Henceforth"—from this very time—"there is laid up for me a crown of righteousness, which the Lord, the Righteous Judge, shall give me at that day, and not to me only, but to all them who love his appearing."

It is not certain that Paul had wholly abandoned the views of his earlier life relative to the second coming of Christ: he probably had not; but it is certain that he refers to the appearing of his Lord now more in the sense implied by Christ in his parables than in the sense implied in his own letters to the Thessalonians. Like the wise virgins he was watching for his Lord, and ready to receive him, having fought a good fight, and having finished the course, and having kept the faith. His dying faith sees no half-way place between him and the society of his Saviour. There was with him no sundering of the man into parts, one part to decay in the ground for ages, and the other to wander, meanwhile, a shapeless, naked ghost, in some intermediate place of conscious existence, only partially enjoying the beatitudes of the future life. To inject such a sentiment into this language of holy triumph would be to rob it of every element of beauty and comfort. As it stands, it expresses the devoted martyr's faith that the man Paul was not only ready for the sacrifice, but that the crown was for *him*. "There is laid up for *me*, a crown."

We can better appreciate this declaration of faith in the dying hour by placing it by the side of Paul's own language when purposely discussing the question of death and immortality. He says, in the fourth chapter of Second Corinthians: "For we know that if our earthly house of this tabernacle were dissolved, we *have* a building of God, a house not made with hands, eternal in the heavens." Such a declaration of opinion on such a subject, made when writing directly upon it, is worth a thousand remote allusions to the probable coming of Christ, to take vengeance upon his enemies and to reward his friends, as defining Paul's views of the mode of man's immortality.

Here he says, the body is merely an earthly house, a temporary tabernacle, a tent for a wayfaring man, but no part of the man himself; but when this is dissolved by death, we have a building of God, a house not made with hands, essentially different from this tabernacle. This is temporary, that is eternal; this is earthly, that is in heaven; a building of God—our home. Let it be borne in mind that the apostle says: We *have*, not that we shall have away down in the ages to come. The entire context is of the same import. To be unclothed of the earthly is to be clothed upon with the heavenly; to depart is to be with Christ. What a beautiful supplement this is to the lengthy discussion on the same subject in the fifteenth chapter of the former epistle, while that discussion beautifies and corroborates this. "It *is sown* in corruption, *it is raised* in incorruption, *it is dissolved* a natural body, *it is renewed* a spiritual body." We lay off an earthly house, we take on a building of God—all in the present tense.*

There is something touchingly beautiful in the dying moments of Stephen. Amidst a shower of stones, he looked steadfastly into heaven and saw the glory of God, and Jesus standing at the right hand of God; and he died saying: "Lord Jesus, receive my spirit." There is here no allusion to a heathen *Hades* as a half-way place between earth and Heaven, but his vision caught a glimpse of the Father and the Son in *Heaven*,

---

* There is much plausibility in the conjecture that our spirit-life is to be attained by the rising of a spirit-form from the earthly house at the moment of death, so resembling the earthly form as to be readily recognizable by the eye of spirit, and often by genuine clairvoyance. There are instances innumerable in which the dying have recognized and spoken to those who had died long before, and many instances, well authenticated, where the dead have appeared to distant acquaintances almost at the instant of their departure, and a long time before the news of their death had reached them in the ordinary channel. Possibly, in the ages not far remote, clairvoyance may be reduced to something like a science, which may not only confirm the fact of man's immortality, but throw some light upon the mode. Its facts are not, even now, to be dismissed with a sneer, or to be treated as exceptional phenomena confined to the illiterate or the superstitious.

and to them, and not to the society of naked ghosts, he expected to go.

The most remarkable feature of this dying scene was the unvailing of the soul, the unclothing of the real man, while yet that soul, the real man, could communicate through fleshly organs with those around. It was not through fleshly eyes that he saw the glory of God, and Jesus standing at the right hand of God, but with the eyes of the spirit man. This he called the opening of Heaven, but it was only the opening of the vail which so thinly intervenes between that fair country and those who, like Stephen, are watching and waiting for the appearance of their Master, whether he come by violence, or by the slower steps of disease. It was an experience too, which was not to be confined to Stephen, but all along the ages it has been often repeated in the death of those who have died in the Lord; showing that Heaven is not, locally, so very far away, and that the man goes at once into the society of the blest, and of God, and of Christ, without the intervention of any intermediate place.*

---

* We find the following beautiful and *Scriptural* paragraph in the work of the late Bishop D. W. Clark, entitled, *Man all Immortal.* It is, indeed, in very uncongenial company, seeing that the object of the book is to prove the resurrection of the material body. If this extract be true, his arguments, though a thousand fold stronger to prove a bodily resurrection, must vanish as mist before the rising sun. This *is true,* as well as beautiful, and the chilly sentence which introduces it cannot neutralize it, nor the pages of argument which follow disprove it.

Anticipating its fatal effect on his unscriptural and unreasonable argument, he says, by way of apology: "It is generally admitted that the full consummation of bliss is not realized till the resurrection." Admitted by whom, forsooth? By those who are conscious that their resurrection dogma is in the face of such plain Scriptural truths, but not by Paul, nor Stephen, nor John, nor Peter, *nor by any dying saint!* This is the paragraph:

"The righteous dead are represented as being *with Christ.* Such

We say that such experiences, though comparatively rare, are not wanting in the common walks of Christian life. Thousands and tens of thousands of dying Christians have, in like manner, not with clouded reason nor excited imagination, but in the calm of a triumphant death, recognized the presence of former loved ones and of other spiritual beings, either angels or the angel-like appearance of the just made perfect, all unseen by others, but unmistakably present to the unvailed eye of immortality. We need not give instances. They might lack authenticity, with those especially who are determined by their chilly faith to put off the day of reunion to that

---

seems to have been the view of the first martyr when he cried, 'Lord Jesus, receive my spirit.' Such also seemed to be the view of Paul, when he expressed a desire to be [not in the place of separate spirits, somewhere this side, but] with Christ, which is far better. And, again, when not only speaking for himself, but for the great body of believers, he says, 'Therefore, we are always confident, knowing that whilst we are at home in the body, we are absent from the Lord. We are confident, I say, and willing rather to be absent from the body *and to be present with the Lord.*' The apostle here expresses the strongest conviction that believers, *from the moment of death*, instead of being in a *separate place* are *with the Lord.* But where is the Lord? Most certainly he has not only ascended on high, but He has entered INTO HEAVEN ITSELF. From these facts it is clearly evident that death ushers the believers into the immediate and glorious presence of Christ.

'One gentle sigh their fetter breaks,
We scarce can say they are gone,
Before the willing spirit takes
Her mansion near the throne.'

How consoling such a truth! To know that we shall be with Christ sweetens the bitterness of the dying agony. Death removes us from our kindred here, but it *brings us into the presence of that friend who is dearer than any brother.*" *Page* 191.

To all of which we most heartily say Amen! But where is left any bodily resurrection, if this be true? The italics and capitals and brackets are all the bishop's. It will not answer to say that the writer predicated all this of the soul as only a part of the man. He speaks of "the righteous dead." "Death ushers the believers." "Believers, from the moment of death, &c."

remote and ever-receding hour, when the sea shall give up the bodies which have fallen into it, and the grave shall restore the bodies which it has covered. Every neighborhood of Christians and every age has furnished repeated examples of such visions, in the death of mature Christians; as if the Father and the Son would not leave us without witnesses of the early and permanent joys of the spirit land.

Nor is the idea of a continued personal existence peculiar to Jacob, or David, or Abraham, or Paul, or Stephen. In spite of the demoralizing tendency of that unscriptural and unreasonable doctrine which separates man into parts, at death, and sends one part to dust, and thence through thousands of successive material changes, until a loud trumpet shall arrest its career; and which sends the other part to some vast receptacle of naked ghosts, there to be half-happy, or half-miserable, until the other part shall rejoin it, man instinctively clings to the Scriptural doctrine of a continuous life when required to apply his notions of immortality to himself. The genuine Christian man's faith is better than his creed, when that intervenes between himself and heaven, and he bids defiance to the great gulf which superstition and the traditions of men had fixed between him and the truth. Like Paul and Stephen, he seizes the immortal at once, however much his education and former mode of thinking might have led him to a different conclusion in health.

We appeal to the experience of every one who has parted with loved ones who died in the hope of a blessed immortality, to say if foremost in their thoughts of them is not that they are with Christ: not in some inferior sense, but in the fullness of heavenly bliss? There was, indeed, a preciousness in their bodily forms, through which alone we had held intercourse with them, which made us consign those bodies to the tomb with reluctance, even after they became offensive to our senses; but there was something of the same tenderness towards the clothing they had worn; and many an unused drawer often discloses to the heart that refuses to be comforted the little stockings or half-worn shoes of the angel-babe, or the garments of the more advanced in years, still sacred because of their former association with the loved and lost. It would not be strange that for the moment we both hoped and desired to see that form again, as we had already arranged to preserve many mementoes of the departed; but time effaces that longing, while the union with the immortal grows stronger as we draw nearer to it by advancing age, and other indications of a speedy reunion.

There is even in the forms of speech of the dying Christian, all so nearly identical in purport, an argument which is not to be despised. The young and the old, the learned and the illiterate, all ignore that vast hiatus which the creeds of men have interposed between earth and heaven.

A few years ago the talented Dr. Olin retired from his class in the Wesleyan University to linger a few months and die. During the early part of his last sickness, while yet able to walk the room, a sweet child of his, some two years of age, sickened and sank rapidly. One day it beckoned to the father to take it up. He took it in his arms and walked a few times across the room when his failing strength admonished him that he must lay it in the crib again. Just as he was doing so the prattler said: "Pa, kiss baby!" He kissed it tenderly. Then it added, "God, take baby!" and in a moment the struggle was over. God had taken the sweet one, answering its request as promptly and tenderly as the earthly father had in giving the final kiss. Let it not be said that this was the utterance of a precocious child, or a mere coincidence; rather let us say that it was the All-Father perfecting praise in one of his little ones, revealing to it things which are hidden from many of the wise and prudent of earth.

A few weeks later the crisis came with the father himself, and he knew that within a few hours more he must die. He had been a believer in the doctrine of a future general resurrection, and for aught that we know he was then, in theory; but how was he in its application to his personal faith? Did he call his friends around him and descant on the glories of the resurrection morning, and point to the time far, far distant, when he and his beloved child and the wife of his youth, now soon to become a widow, should be brought up from the sleep of ages? Not he. Calling his wife to him in a moment of calmness and serenity, he said: "I am about to die. In a few days you will lay this body in the grave; but do not say that you have buried your husband. *Your husband will be in heaven!*"

This was no precocious child, using language which it did not understand. It was no obscure, illiterate, excitable creature, half crazed by opiates. It was the great Olin, the cultivated scholar, the mature Christian, leaping, in his dying faith, every gulf which superstition and tradition had wrongfully interposed between him and the society of his babe, and of his Redeemer; and expressing, in well-weighed language, the same faith which Paul and Stephen had uttered in their dying hours.

The closing hours of the late Dr. Cookman, of New York, were replete with instruction and comfort. For days and weeks his conversation, as it related to the near approach of death indicated the triumph of one whose life was hid with Christ in God. A few hours before his death, calling his wife to his bed-side, he informed her that he had just had a glorious vision. Though it seemed much like a dream, he knew that it was not a dream, for he was awake. He had seen his father, and brother, and child, and many other former companions of life, each of whom had bidden him welcome to the mansion prepared for him in the better world. His account of the interviews was calm and circumstantial. They had evidently been, to him, realities. Is not such an incident light from experience, which we dare not ignore in our inquiry into the mode of man's immortality? Those who insist that heaven is a far-away country, inclosed with jasper walls, within which a part of the man is imprisoned, semi-happy, until after some future general resurrection, will not deny the fact; but they assume that the soul—only a part of the man—was *sent* from that far-away home on a special mission for this special occasion. We prefer the more Scriptural and rational explanation of this, and of thousands upon thousands of similar experiences, which assumes that the soul is the man, and that these *men* were just what they seemed to the dying Cookman to be. Dying, they had been unclothed of the mortal, material, earthy body and they had put on immortality, and so were ever with the Lord, and like him. They *were* as he *is*, they *are now* as he *is*, with a spiritual body fashioned from a physical body, if Christ exists now in that form, but not otherwise. But their natural bodies had decomposed in the sea and in the grave. The honored father's body had gone to ocean depths with the ill-fated steamer thirty years before, while the bodies of the others had been buried with the usual care, yet here were these *men* communing with this *man.* Their spiritual bodies had not been made from earthly bodies, yet they had spiritual bodies, easily recognized by the dying man.

Of course we cannot prove that the appearances of those loved ones was not an exceptional visit but a habitual presence, and that they became visible to the dying man as the chariots and horsemen of Israel did to the servant of Elijah, and as the person of Jesus did to the dying Stephen; but the contrary is equally beyond the possibility of demonstration. To the conception of the writer these unnumbered instances of spirit-recognition are utterly irreconcilable with that theory of future life which sends the soul, as only a part of the man, at death "far, far away," to a land from which there is no return, except when *sent* occasionally. *Our* dead are ever living, and ever-present, though unseen.

A few hours later he said to his son: "I have been sweeping by the gates all day," unconsciously and without premeditation using the language of the dying to indicate his notion of a continued personal existence. Did any dying man ever speak of being sundered into parts? It is always I, myself, my personal existence.

The late venerable Dr. Guthrie, of Scotland, was a theoretical believer in the traditional faith of his church, as to a future general resurrection, yet, like ten thousands of others, in his better faith he often broke the shackles and stood above the dogma, unwittingly renouncing it. Said he, not long before his death, in one of his eloquent flights of personal faith, "They tell me I am old. It is not so. I am as young to-day as ever I was. It is true these knees are becoming feeble, and these limbs are somewhat palsied, and these eyes are growing dim; but these eyes are not I, myself, these limbs are not I, myself, this is only the house in which I now live. But it will soon be taken down, then I will appear in another and a better house."

When Dr. McLean was dying, he said: "I can now contemplate clearly the grand scene *to which I am going.*"

"Dr. Payson wrote to a friend just before dying: "I might date this letter from the land of Beulah, of which I have been some weeks a happy inhabitant. The celestial city is full in view. Its glories beam upon me; its breezes fan me; its odors are wafted to me; its sounds strike my ears, and its spirit is breathed into my heart. Nothing separates *me* from it but the river of death, which now appears but an insignificant rill, which may be crossed at a single step."

Dr. Lowell Mason, the sweet singer, died recently at an advanced age. Long years ago, he had buried his first born, a lovely boy, named Daniel. Friends stood around him watching the ebbing out of life, at the close of a beautiful Sabbath, but all oblivious to the living, whom he loved tenderly, and of whom he had just taken his final farewell, the dying man opened his eyes, and looking upward intently, said: "Daniel, may I come?" and then with a smile of recognition, he added: "Let me come," and breathed his last.

"I thought last night I was in heaven," said

a dying Christian lady, the wife of Rev. J. S. Barwick, the day before her death; "and so captivated was I with what I heard and saw, that the vision has not yet faded away nor is the charm broken. I wonder if indeed I was not there." Most certainly she was, just as Paul was, there, "out of the body."

We might multiply these examples into volumes, all tending to show that the language of the dying Christian seldom, if ever, refers to the doctrine of a future general resurrection, but like that of Paul and Stephen, nearly always apprehends an immediate home in the land of immortals, whatever may have been their theory in health.

And it is no answer to the argument which we draw from these facts that all Christians believe that the soul, meaning only a part of the man, goes to heaven. In these hours of Christian triumph the soul becomes the man, and the body enters no more into the account than do the treasures of earth which are exchanged for the bliss of immortality.

We have given elsewhere an extract from the book of the late Bishop D. W. Clark, beautifully expressing his faith in the immediate entrance of "the righteous dead" into heaven, *where Christ is.* We shall hereafter give another gem from the same book expressive of his belief that the dead are often with the living. These two sentiments blended indicate, as we show elsewhere, that heaven is not, locally, so "far, far away" as is generally supposed, leaving also, to our notion, not the least possible vestige of a bodily resurrection, although they are strangely enough found in a book devoted largely to the defense of that dogma.

Bishop Clark has since died. The approach

of death was so gradual and unmistakable that he had abundant occasion to speak of the power of his faith to give him victory over it, and many were the words of comfort which he gave to his family and friends, but none are more precious than these: "Our separation will not be a complete one. I feel that *I* shall often be with you. *I* cannot speak words to you, but God, in his tenderness and loving-kindness, will permit *me* to suggest beautiful thoughts to you, and lead your minds heavenward. This idea is very present with me."

Later, and only a few hours before his death, he said, as he seemed to realize, even now, the society of heaven: "Tireless company! Tireless song! The song of the angels is a glorious song. It thrills my ears even now. *I* am going to join the angels' song."

Here is an eminent Christian scholar who was never excitable, and who never expressed his ideas loosely, ignoring the creed and, like the dying Paul, rising above his former opinions, and in the sublimity of Christian triumph entering at once into heaven, yet hovering around the loved of life, suggesting, by spirit communings, as he says in his book, "beautiful thoughts, and leading their minds heavenward." See how he says, *me*, *my*, *I*, my personal self, not a mere fragment of a man.

Long years ago, though it seems but yesterday, the writer of this book was called upon to suffer his first great bereavement in the death of his first born, a lovely boy three years of age. The day before his departure the little fellow asked, with child-like simplicity: "Ma, will the angels open the gates for me as soon as I get there?" "Why do you ask that?" said the anxious mother. "Because I am going to be an angel," was the prompt reply; this little untaught one shrinking instinctively or by inspiration from the idea so cherished by many men of ripe years and profound scholarship, of remaining outside of the city of God, even for an instant. No one but parents who have been stricken in like manner can realize the grief of that hour of separation, and no one who has not faith in the immediate immortality of the dead can even remotely imagine the sweet bliss which mingled with the tears of sorrow, as the bereaved parents said, while closing the eyes of the departed: "He has already received an answer to his interesting question. The gates *are* open for him. He *is* with the Lord, 'for of such is the kingdom of heaven.'"

In the room where these lines are written, so recently that the fragrance of the hour yet lingers, a daughter, just entering the maturity of womanhood, was called to die. Calmly and patiently, through months of intense suffering, she approached the final hour with many expressions of trust in God which would have done honor to a war-worn veteran. The last day finally came, after a night of indescribable pain: cold limbs, a failing pulse, and difficult breathing all indicated the closing scene. Addressing her mother, she said: "You will not have to watch with me to-night, for this poor, suffering body will be at rest, but I shall be with my Saviour." Shortly afterwards, having taken an affectionate farewell of the family, she reached out her hand, cold in death, as if to embrace some one unseen by the rest. With a smile of recognition she began to call by name departed members of the family, and others of her acquaintances who had died, adding, after some minutes of such greetings: "Here we are, an unbroken family in heaven, washed in the blood of the Lamb. Washed, washed, washed!" and in a few moments she was in the spirit-world.*

Is it any unwarrantable deduction from these scenes (and they are by no means of infrequent occurrence) that the dead live, and that they

---

* We do not object to classifying such phenomena as this recognition of friends under the general head of clairvoyance, although so little is known of that mental or spiritual perception which is called by this name. Its moral lesson will suffer nothing by such classification, for the joyousness of such visions is never granted to others than those who die in the Lord. The facts of clairvoyance are yet too few and too detached to establish any doctrine by them, while they are too many and too well authenticated to be wholly ignored in any investigation of mind in the body, or spirit out of the body. There may be much more in it than we are willing to believe, while there is too little to command our assent to all its pretensions.

The properties of electricity and of the magnet were, until recently, quite as mysterious. Who shall say that some Franklin or Morse may not yet utilize, in some unexpected way, the half-known but wholly unintelligible laws of spirit?

We only add, in this connection, that while such visions are frequent with the dying, while they can yet communicate with us through the ordinary channels, there are instances, which are entitled to the utmost credence, of natural clairvoyants witnessing not only the spirits of other departed ones in the room, but that of the dying joining the group and departing together. We can not comprehend how this is, and, while we believe that it has occurred, we cannot prove it to the incredulous; hence we do not introduce it as an argument for others, although it has an influence on our own mind. We believe, with Paul, that we *have* a spiritual house; in other words, that the soul is the man, and that when it leaves—when *we* leave—the body we are with the Lord, and clothed at once with our house which is heavenly—with a shape and form, a perfectly distinct organization, a *body* if you please, though it be not made of clay as these bodies are. Far hence be the notion, entertained not only by the illiterate, but by some men of education, that the spirit is without body or parts, a mere shapeless bit of gas or ether! There is neither philosophy, nor experience, nor revelation in any such a notion, and the sooner it is wholly discarded the sooner the world will begin to learn something of the mode of man's immortality, from the light of experience.

live in forms that are recognizable by spirit? Such visions, so oft repeated, and so well authenticated, constitute as legitimate a source of knowledge in reference to the mode of man's immortality as anything in the Bible itself. They are beautiful illustrations of the language of Christ: "I *am* the resurrection and the life, and whosoever believeth in me shall never die." Such a faith, and such departures, divest the farewell of every ingredient of death. It is no death, it is rather life begun.

There 's no such thing as death,
  To those who live aright;
'Tis but the racer casting off
  What most impedes his flight.
'Tis but one little act
  Life's drama must contain,
One struggle, keener than the rest,
  And then an end of pain.

There 's no such thing as death,
  That which is thus miscalled
Is life escaping from the chains
  That have so long enthralled.
'Tis a once-hidden star
  That pierces through the night,
To shine in gentle radiance forth
  Amid its kindred light.

There 's no such thing as death,
  In nature nothing dies,
From each sad remnant of decay
  Some forms of life arise;
The faded leaf that falls,
  All sere and brown to earth,
Ere long will mingle with the shapes
  That give the floweret birth.

There 's no such thing as death,
  'Tis but the blossom spray,
Dropping before the coming fruit
  That seeks the summer's ray,
'Tis but the bud displaced
  Before the perfect flower.
'Tis only faith exchanged for sight,
  And weariness to power.

CHAPTER XIV.

Common Theories of the Resurrection Examined.

THE scope of this discussion does not contemplate controversy. Our design has been to state the doctrine of man's immortality, as we find it taught in the Bible, and as illustrated by experience and science so far as these sources of light can furnish any information upon the subject, with as little reference to the opinions of others as would be consistent with a perfect understanding of the question. Least of all have we intended to array what men may call science against the teachings of revelation. There can be no antagonism between science and revelation. Any seeming difference must result from a misunderstanding of one or the other, or of both.

Having seen how the absolutely universal opinions of former ages upon some Bible questions have been utterly overthrown by the Biblical and scientific research of a later period, dare any one assume that we have attained the *ultima thule* of knowledge on any subject? Is it impious to submit any dogma of religion or philosophy to a new investigation? In the light of past experience, is there either sense or argument in parading even "the unanimous assent" of this age, or any former age, in behalf of any doctrine of morals or of science?

It is proper, perhaps, to briefly examine some of the more common theories of men on the subject of a literal bodily resurrection. We say theories, for most who have written in behalf of this dogma have felt it incumbent upon them to devise some easy way for its accomplishment, seeing that Paul had neglected or refused to do so necessary a thing.

Humanly speaking, it is not a thing incredible for God to raise the dead, as Christ was raised, to whose resurrection the apostle referred when he confronted the judge with this proposition, but it is incredible that He should carry out any of the many programmes of those who believe that the earthly bodies of men, after undergoing the endless mutations of ages, shall be rebuilt and then reanimated by the soul's returning from heaven or hell, or from some half-way place, and that the man, thus completed, shall be again returned to happiness or misery, to finish an eternity of joy or woe, suitably intensified by this reunion.

The shades of difference between the theorists who thus undertake to tell us how the Almighty will do this incredible thing are almost endless. And no wonder. Having no common basis, and the most indefinite common notion of the result, they war against each other as much as against the truth; agreeing in only the one idea that there is to be, at what they are pleased to call the end of the world, a resurrection of the bodies of men—the actual flesh and bones of this life.

We assume that the resurrection of dead bodies is incredible, because it implies a constant infraction of every known law of matter, and because God has never indicated, by revelation or by his works, that he would do this strange thing. If there was any analogy in nature, or any promise in revelation. we would gladly accept the Word of God as conclusive against all human incredulity or human weakness; but there is neither.

It is a favorite argument with those who teach a literal resurrection of the body, to hunt up analogies; but every one they find turns against their doctrine. The return of day after the darkness of night is one favorite analogy. But night is not death. The sun does not die when it goes down. It is not an inapt illustration of man's continuous existence, for

> " The sun that sets
> Beyond the western wave is not extinct.
> It brightens in another hemisphere,
> And gilds another region with its rays,"

as the soul, the man, ceasing to live on earth, lives in the land of immortality.

The return of spring is often eloquently paraded, if not as an argument, yet as an apt illustration of the resurrection of the bodies of men. Alas! nothing which dies in autumn ever lives again in the spring. There is a live germ, or a live root, or a live stock, which puts on beauty on the return of spring, but the dead leaf or the dead branch, like the dead body, never lives again. It may illustrate the continuous existence of the man which, unclothed of the present body, is clothed upon with the heavenly, but it sheds no light upon the future life of dead bodies.

The change from caterpillar to butterfly is often referred to as almost divine in its teaching. But the dead caterpillar never becomes a butterfly. The shell of the living caterpillar never lives again, after the vital part escapes as a butterfly. There is in this change no death to the insect, but only to its rougher tabernacle. This transition from a lower to a higher mode of life may not inaptly illustrate the escape of the soul, the real man, from its earthly form, but it gives no countenance to the revival of the body thus abandoned, for the caterpillar never returns to the house it left. It is content with the more beautiful butterfly life. The dead "slug" never lives again.

The foundation truth of all which relates to man has already been noticed. It is that the soul, the spirit, the mind, is the man, distinct and separate from the body, which is only the temporary dwelling-place of the man. We think that we have shown in the second chapter of this book that the most rational construction which can be placed upon the Mosaic account of creation is in accordance with this view. And after all, this is the common rational view which all the more intelligent Christians take, though all may not have the same method of stating it, and some may at times even argue that the body, too, is a part of the man. Bishop Ames recently expressed this idea in his own inimitable style when speaking of an old man: "It is true his hair grows thin, but the hair is not *he;* his eyesight may be less keen than in earlier manhood, but the eye is not *he;* the hearing may be a little dull, but that is not *he;* HE is *within*, and the real *he* is ever youthful."

This *form* of man, this curiously wrought piece of machinery which we call the body, or the earthly house of this tabernacle, originally made of the dust of the ground, is purely material, and the particles of matter used in its construction lose none of the properties of matter by being employed in constituting a human body.

The fact that this machinery is so constituted as to propagate its species does not, so far as reason or revelation shows, change the nature of the matter thus used.

It is the same to-day. We eat, and drink, and breathe, and the matter thus taken into the body becomes a part of the body through the operations of the "wonderfully made" machinery of our physical structure. During the first years of life some of this is appropriated to growth, in our addition to supplying the waste which from childhood is going on. For a few years more it barely supplies the waste, and maintains the man in the vigor of manhood. After a while it cannot do even that much, and the man fails in strength and size, until decrepitude foretells death. In some cases this machinery, working badly, produces deformity. It may result in distressing obesity, or in inconvenient leanness, or some malformation may be indicated by rickets, or humpback, or lameness.

We know that from childhood to the grave there is a constant change in the material of which the body is composed. Men dare not sleep in close, small rooms, lest the matter which has once done its work in the body and has escaped through the lungs and pores return to damage the system. It is this law of decay which makes crowded churches and lecture-rooms unwholesome without suitable ventilation. Waste or decay is a universal law of organized matter, for the repair of which food is taken and digested, to be in its turn cast off as effete.

Now, it is a thing incredible that God should attach such importance to the matter that may have been at any time a part of a man that he takes special care of it, and ultimately gathers it all together, that it may be "reinfused" by the soul, and live for ever in an unchangeable state. It is incredible, because to gather together all the matter which may have constituted any given man's body during an ordinary average life would, as a simple, inevitable, undeniable fact, make a huge, unwieldy mass for the resurrection body.

To avoid this undesirable result—we do not say absurdity, for that does not mean anything with a man who accepts the dogma of the resurrection in its popular sense, since he defies all reason in reaching his conclusion, and gravely answers that the resurrection is above human comprehension—but to avoid such an undesirable, not to say improbable, result, and to make the resurrection body a model of beauty and proportion, the crippled, and the deformed, and the old having been all recast, it is gravely assumed by men of no less note than the late Bishop Kingsley, that this difficulty is surmounted by claiming that the body to be raised is not the matter which has belonged to the man through life, and been from time to time thrown off as waste, but simply the body that died. That died when, forsooth? Every vital action is death itself. Every breath we exhale carries away dead matter. It is only when the dead matter of the body is promptly dismissed that the man enjoys good health. A healthy man does not die daily, but he dies constantly, so far as the body is concerned. When can it be said that the man died who had wasted away from robust manhood to a mere skeleton, because the vital processes had, for a season, thrown off more dead matter than they had taken on new from the usual source of supply? What is the specific article of death to such a person, but the conclusion of a process of death which had had the better of the vital processes for weeks, or months, or years? Is only that remnant of a body the body which dies? and shall that which died last week, or last month, or last year have no affinity for this last remnant? Why should this remnant be more sacred than its fellow particles of earth of the same origin and of precisely the same nature, which had once, with it, constituted the body of the man?

The accretions of flesh and bone which build up the man from the child are regarded by those who believe in a resurrection of the natural body as legitimate matter from which to construct the future resurrection body, but when the imperfect workings of the wonderful machinery take on a superabundance of fat, or muscle, or lymph, and the person becomes a monster, all dropsical and deformed by the unhealthy accretions, it becomes the province of the resurrection to eliminate all this superabundance of matter, though to the test of science every particle of that monster is like every other particle in its ultimate constituents, and the great chemist—Decay—preys alike upon all.

Amputation sometimes removes at an instant half or more of the material structure, perhaps already putrid and offensive. Does that remain any more a part of the man than if an equal amount had been removed by disease? If not, then the body which dies may die legless or armless; and must not the resurrection body be the same, if only the body which dies is raised? If not, why not?

If the subject were one upon which we were allowed to reason, the fact that in the endless mutations of matter it must often happen that a portion of the body of one man becomes a part of the body of another, as when one man eats another, or when a man eats a fish which had eaten a man, might suggest a difficulty: but this possibility of confusion is dismissed by the believers in the doctrine, by referring the whole subject to the unexplained mysteries of God's unknown laws.

Pursuing this subject with such results, and being confronted, though not answered, by such a reference, gives poignancy to the satire of the lecturer in the law school who informed his pupils that lawyers must become better logicians than preachers, for legal sophistry could be exposed and its conclusions overthrown by the better argument, while the preacher, vanquished, could retreat behind: "Great is the mystery of godliness," and be safe.

The discussion of this subject has, however, driven the advocates of a future general resurrection to numerous explanations to get rid of obvious objections to it, from the standpoint of reason and science. One, giving many good reasons why the resurrection can not apply to the bodies of men at all, yet clinging to the tradition of a general resurrection at some future "last day," and to the idea of a compound existence, a soul and a body, as man, sends the soul to *Hades* at death, where it is to remain until the end of the world, whatever that is, when it will be "resurrected," and sent to Paradise or perdition, according as it has been good or bad in life.

The principal proof of such a position is the supposition that the Bible says that Christ went and preached to the spirits in *Hades* immediately after his crucifixion, whereas, according to appointment with the thief, he went directly to Paradise. But this theory assumes that there is a good end and a bad end of that underworld, separated by a great gulf, and that Christ accompanied the penitent thief as far as the Paradise department, and then crossed over the gulf to preach to those who had been disobedient in the days of Noah. After this he returned to the upper world, in time to be present at the resurrection of his body. To our mind this seems like the most reprehensible trifling.

This manufacturing of a place for departed spirits, and dividing into compartments for the convenience of the different kinds of spirits, is not altogether new; but to make the resurrection apply to bringing up spirits from the "vasty deep" is rather a novel way of getting rid of the objections to a bodily resurrection, by plunging into greater absurdities, if possible.

The endless changes of matter, from one body to another, and the possibility of its becoming a part of many bodies, are facts fatal to the idea of a literal resurrection, and have given rise to many conjectures and theories. One is, that God has made it a universal law of matter, that when it has once been in a human form *at the hour of death* it never can become any part of any other human body. This is assuming a law for matter which is not known to exist, but which is known not to exist, for human flesh is identical in all its essential properties with all other flesh, is derived from the same material, through the same process, and is acted upon by gastric juices and other solvents, the same as other flesh.

CHAPTER XV.

Further Objections to the Common Theories of a Bodily Resurrection.

AS a matter of fact, we know that in many cases men have eaten other men, to say nothing of the remoter facts alluded to in the former chapter. How then can it be truly said, that the matter which composes one human body can never become a part of another body? This absurd assumption can be maintained only by the further absurdity, that only a small part of what every man regards as his body is really his body, and that all else is mere foreign matter. Any doctrine of science, or morals, or religion, which depends upon such an outrage upon the common sense of mankind, cannot command the respect of thinking men.

The trimmings of our nails, or of our hair, which we so unceremoniously throw away, were, only a few months ago, food in our mouths, and had reached a fitness for this ignominious destiny through what we call "growth," which is only a comprehensive word for the action upon that food, of the stomach and its juices and the other parts of the machinery of this wonderful structure. While eliminating the matter which became nails and hair, that same machinery had separated from the same food other particles which were dismissed from the body without the aid of scissors or knife, some being cast off through the lungs, some through sensible or insensible perspiration, some through the urinary organs, and some, not well adapted to passing again to the outer-world through either the lungs, or the kidneys, or the pores of the skin, is "cast out into the draught."

Can any good reason be given why any one portion of this waste ever was more truly a part of the body than any other portion? That it took longer for a given portion of food to fulfill its mission and escape to the outer-world through nail or hair than it took another portion to reach the same fate through the lungs, or the skin, or otherwise, makes that matter no more sacred than this, nor any more a part of the body while *in transitu.* Neither bone nor muscle, blood nor lymph, is exempt from the law of accretion and excretion. Every part of the body takes on new particles from every meal that is eaten, and continues to cast off its effete matter to make room for the new.

Can any such matter, having a common origin, and all tending to a common destiny, be held to be more sacred and honorable than any other part? The cornea of the eye, or the enamel of the teeth, is of the cold, lifeless earth, and passes in common with other portions to the same end.

Physiologists agree that the phenomenon called digestion begins immediately upon the entrance of the food into the mouth of a healthy man, although some minutes elapse before the work has progressed sufficiently to be appreciable by the tests usually applied; hence, it at once becomes as truly a part of the body of the man as it ever becomes. The future blood, and bone, and muscle, are indeed only *in embryo,* but they are there, and that food is no longer bread or meat, but flesh, and bone, and tissue, in a forming state, which began when the food was masticated and mixed with the secretions of the mouth. The gray mass which issues from between the upper and the nether millstones is neither flour nor bran, but it is no longer wheat. The manufacture of flour began in the mastication of the wheat, as the manufacture of bone and flesh began when a like process was undergone by the food in the mouth.

If it is proper to call flesh or bone a part of the body, it is proper to so call the blood. If the blood is a part of the body, so is chyle; if chyle is, so is chyme; if chyme is, so, also, is the partly digested food just swallowed. That which is left after the separation of the chyle is technically called excrement, because it is generally more speedily passed out of the system, but, until it has passed, it is in truth, no more excrement than that which enters into the blood, nor is it any the less a part of the body. Much of that which is thought to be so vital because it becomes blood, is excreted through the kidneys, and the lungs, and the pores of the skin, and is sent to the outer-world long before this so-called excrement reaches its destiny through its channel. Indeed, every particle of bone, and flesh, and blood, becomes excrement in its turn, and passes away; hence the excrements have all been a part of the body, for all parts become excrement.

Even the effete matter yet within the body is as truly a part of the body as that employed in the vital processes, for we cannot conceive of a healthy body without its due proportion of effete matter in the lungs, in the intestines and in all the other channels of escape, more or less ready to leave the body to make room for its new and vital successor. Besides, much of that which is vital to one part of the body is effete as to another part. Having served its purpose in its former capacity, and having departed to give place to a fresher portion, it stops, so to speak, to vitalize and rejuvenate a later if not a lower class of organs, or parts of the body.

Because a given portion of bone-making matter is effete as to blood, is it not a part of the body? Is effete bone, passing through muscle and tissue, probably giving life and strength to them in turn, no longer a part of the body? It is certain that what we choose to call effete matter, in itsproper place, waiting only for a proper time to be discharged, is as necessary to a healthy action of the parts as that which we call vital matter. In short, our body is just what we see it. The bony structure is not the body, the fleshy structure is not the body, the nervous structure is not the body, but all these, combined with every other portion, constitute the body. A body may be sadly diseased, yet it is a body. It may have an undue proportion of effete matter—it may be nearly decayed—nay, it may be effete in death, yet it is a body.

Hence, the body of one man may become a part of the body of another man, and often does; and the objection which such a fact constitutes against a future resurrection of fleshly bodies is well taken, and is entitled to all the force that fact can give.

Among the latest attempts to reconcile the theory of a literal bodily resurrection with the known laws of science is that of Dr. Joseph H. Wythe. It brings scientific discoveries to bear upon the difficulties which science has suggested.

As it is fresh, if not altogether new, we quote the following:

"Much of the matter connected with our bodies, during life, is doubtless foreign, and not essential to their identity. Nine-tenths of the human body consists of water, as has been shown by the weight of a corpse which had been desiccated in an oven, and of the remaining tenth part much is material in a state of decay, having been used by the vital processes and now effete, or being cast off, so that a very small portion of the matter of our bodies can really be said to be our own.*

"We have seen that, of the total amount of material associated with our bodies, physiology shows a very small part only which is in a nascent condition, or which is being applied to vital use, can be said to belong to our bodies. Supposing this small part to be indestructible, many of the objections to a resurrection, drawn from the nourishment of other organized bodies will be removed, for both animals and vegetables are built up from the decomposition of other beings." — *Science and Revelation*, pages 258, 259.

This, it must be remembered, is a contribution from the medical department, and grapples with an objection to the resurrection which is

---

* "Our own," indeed! Whose is it, if it is not ours? Is any part of the body too sacredly ours to be amputated by you doctors? In amputating a leg or two, you would probably take away something that is neither water nor "effete matter." Would any part of that amputated limb still remain "our own"? If the solid portions, why not the liquid portions? And does a portion of the body thus removed by your knife remain any more sacredly "our own" than the portion which is removed by disease or by your drastic medicines? Is there any part of the body which does not, in its turn become effete?

much better disposed of by the divinity doctors. It is far more sensible to assume that if God intends to raise dead bodies, he will take care of them and raise them intact, than to put them in an oven and dry away nine-tenths of them, and then reduce the other tenth largely, by throwing away the "effete matter," and leaving perhaps not over one-twelfth of the man to be raised. The argument is puerile in the extreme, and utterly worthless, further than to show that there is a real scientific difficulty to wrestle with. For if God has made one-twelfth of the body of a man indigestible by other men, he could have made the whole body indigestible. If one-twelfth is indestructible, why may not all be? Besides, this robs the resurrection of all its joys to those who attach importance to the body. If eleven-twelfths of the body are to be dried up in some furnace, or lost in the mutation of matter, let the balance go! It is not the body which we loved, but only a very insignificant part of it, and that all dried up! If that is the best that science can do, give us the preacher's stronghold, "Great is the mystery of godliness," and let us believe without any reason at all, except that we think God has promised it.

We were not so much surprised to find such a bungling apology from a physician as to find it indorsed and amended by Dr. Whedon, in the Methodist *Quarterly Review* for 1872, page 679, thus:

"When the foreign elements are thus eliminated, and the true body remains alone, it is thereby reduced to one-tenth of its apparent magnitude." [Suppose it is, can not God as easily take charge of ten-tenths as of one-tenth?]

"But a still further reduction ensues from the abolition of the alimentary canal and generative parts of the earthly human system, as both reason and the New Testament suggest."

Reason may make such a suggestion to those with whom the wish is father to the thought, but nothing of the kind is suggested in the New Testament. If the New Testament teaches any bodily resurrection at all, it teaches that the entire body will rise, not desiccated nor eliminated. Pray tell us what is left of the body after these two doctors have it ready for the resurrection? One desiccates nine-tenths, and then dismisses ever so much more as "effete matter," and then the other doctor leaves out the alimentary canal, beginning, of course, with the teeth, and including all the absorbent vessels. (And Dr. Whedon knows that, ages ago, this leaving out the digestive organs was repudiated, at least so far as the wicked were concerned, because teeth will be needed for gnashing in the outer darkness which awaits them.) Would not the lungs and heart go too? The liver certainly would. And then the generative parts must go also! By this time there can not be left over one-twentieth part of the man to be raised. Is this small fraction of the body the dear old body which is to be so important that heaven can not be heaven without it? Would it not honor God much more to assume that he can and will raise all that appertains to our present personal existence, so that the body may not only be the identical body, but like the one which is supposed to be so precious? Certainly this is the prevailing idea of those who are not learned enough to know that about nineteen-twentieths of what they have always supposed to be body was only "foreign substances" and unimportant appendages.*

If not this, then let us accept the plain Scriptural notion that the immortal part is the man, and that when that is unclothed of its earthly house it will be at once clothed upon with its house which is from heaven; that, dying, we are with the Lord, and being with him we are like him.

Evidently, reasoning upon the method of the resurrection of this physical body is an up hill business. Science does not cast any light upon it; and the unsophisticated one who believes that God looks down and watches *all* his dust till he shall bid it rise, falling back upon the stronghold, of "the mystery of godliness" for explanation of the mode, is quite as correct as the profound doctors of medicine or divinity who propose to simplify the operation by dispensing with nineteen-twentieths of the body. The old Hebrew notion of an indestructible bone or muscle, which they called *Luz,* is certainly easier than all this, and the germ-theory is not any more absurd.

The arguments which assume the necessity of such a physical resurrection in order to vindicate

---

* This theory of these two doctors was ludicrously though unintentionally demolished, a few months ago, in New Albany, Indiana, in a set sermon intended to prove the resurrection of the body. The preacher, more remarkable for his talent and piety than the beauty of his person, having become wrought up by the inspiration of his theme, clinched his argument (?) by straightening himself up and saying: "Yes, I want to come up, just six feet three in my stockings, gangling, long-armed, squint-eyed J—— W——, just as you see me now." Brave man to thus accept the least desirable absurdity of the theory of a bodily resurrection! Almost any other man would have submitted at least to the straightening of the eyes. We introduce the incident to show that this doctrine of a literal resurrection is yet preached sometimes in respectable pulpits, before intelligent congregations, in its most absurd aspects.

God's justice and perfect our happiness, are almost too absurd to deserve notice, yet they are the most common. Some men are never so happy as when they are looking after other people's motives, and this habit grows on them until they learn to assign a motive to the Almighty for all that he does, whether it be an earthquake, or a Chicago fire, or the pestilence among the horses. His motive for raising this identical body, with all its parts and functions, has not escaped their criticism.

Among the many reasons which must have been uppermost in the mind of the Eternal, they assume, was the fact that man had sinned in this body, and if he had ever repented, he repented in this body, and this body having been a partaker of the sins or the joys of this world, should also be a partaker of the rewards or punishments of another. What part matter, whether dead or alive, can take in transgression, so as to become morally responsible, we have no means of knowing; but on the supposition that matter can sin, we see no reason why the dagger should not be hanged with the arm that wielded it. To such minds there can be no perfect joy in heaven until there is a re-union of the soul with the body, nor can the pains of hell be adequate until the body in which the soul sinned shall be turned into the lake of fire and brimstone, that soul and body may burn together eternally.

Another reason which is often given is the love we have for this body, and the care we take of it, such that the soul cannot be fully happy without it. There is much more force in this than some imagine, for, indisputably, many persons have little joy except that which arises from feeding and adorning their bodies, and a heaven of pure mental or spiritual occupation would be the direst hell that they could imagine.

"I love this old body!" said the preacher in our hearing, when arguing in favor of a literal physical resurrection. We knew that, already, from the care he bestowed upon it; and well he might love it, for it was large and well proportioned, and, in fact, handsome. Moreover, his digestion was good, and few were the pains that he suffered except those of the gout family. But we thought that the same argument would require the resurrection of his coat, for he loved that too, even more than his body, for he polluted this with tobacco, while that was kept as clean and stainless as the most assiduous attention to the brush could keep it. One-half the attention to the mind, the real man, might have made him the model preacher intellectually that he was physically.

And we thought, too, the coat and the body were much nearer kin than he had supposed. The same sheep which, by its curious machinery, had manufactured grass into wool for his outer adornment, had, at the same time, and out of the same grass, manufactured mutton for his inward comfort. The weaver and the tailor had taken the wool in hand and produced that glossy coat, while the butcher and the cook had rendered the mutton palatable, and thus long separated particles of the same sheep had come again into close relationship; but still both coat and body were of the earth, earthy, though they had reached their present relationship to the man through such different processes. Why, then, should not the coat be raised and immortalized with the body?

Some men, like Dr. Wythe, above quoted,

think that so much of a sheep as becomes "our own," by becoming mutton and entering into our bodies, becomes very sacred, while so much of the same sheep, manufactured out of the same grass, as goes into wool and becomes clothing, is only "foreign matter." And they call that science! *

---

* There are some things in the book *Credo* which has just come to our notice, that so clearly dispose of the doctrine of a future bodily resurrection that we take the liberty of further quoting from it, as at least indicating that the train of thought which is found in these pages has found its way into the ranks of eminent teachers, of whom Dr. Townsend is confessedly one. True, the doctor finds himself tethered to much of the figment which he seems heartily to discard. Thus we find this incongruous sentence: "The 'resurrection unto life,' and the 'resurrection unto damnation,' would seem to be meaningless in the lips of Christ, were not the human soul, at some future time, to come into possession of a body, in which it shall live, and through which it shall act." Whereas such phrases are full of meaning, when we remember that Christ says, I *am* the resurrection. I *am* the life. That the dead *are* raised, not will be; and that Paul says we *have* that body upon the dissolution of this. Where, dear Doctor, is there a single passage of Scripture which says that the soul, *at some future time*, shall come into possession of a body? It cannot be found in any man's Bible.

Much more consistent with the teachings of inspiration are these sentences, referring to the doctrine of the fifteenth chapter of First Corinthians: "We are not able to see on what principle these passages can be made to harmonize with the theory of a resurrection, which calls for the restoration of the old body, particle for particle, as it was constituted when it returned to dust." . . . "What is the inevitable conclusion? Is it that the same body which goes into the grave is to come out of it, and that the old material is to be the identical material of the new body? Is not the simple and natural meaning of the passage this—that the old body gives place to a new one?" . . . "Are we to enter these worn-out, diseased bodies again, and bear them through eternity?" . . . "Nay, as we have borne the image of the earthy, we are also to bear the image of the heavenly." . . . "This interpretation of the passages in question relieves us at once from the necessity of employing in our reconstruction the old particles of matter which have lost their identity; which have been organized and reorganized, again and again; which have entered into other bodies, into the vegetable and animal kingdom, into the atmosphere and the clouds that float above us." . . . "We intuitively demand a body which shall be free from the gross materials of the present." . . . We would change tenements, rather than be at the trouble and expense of moving out only to move back again."

It is almost painful to see one who entertains such comforting and Scriptural views of the future life as the foregoing and the following, tethered to the loathsome corpse of medieval superstition, and apparently struggling to be free. No Romish dogma has less foundation in the Bible, or in common sense, or in the deductions which science makes from undoubted spiritual phenomena, than that called the intermediate estate—the assumed half-way place between earth and heaven. Romanists need it for their purgatorial purifications, but enlightened Christians should discard it at once and forever. But for an occasional ungracious allusion to it, one would suppose that our author had risen entirely above it, entering into the purer atmosphere of the teachings of Christ and his apostles. The following beautiful sentences belong to a higher plane than that to which Professor Townsend seems to have attained, yet they are found in his "Credo": "Is it not true that there is an instinctive and positive demand in every human nature, for a body to dwell in? Who can think of the future life with pleasure without thinking of it as organized? The idea of a purely spiritual existence unembodied, thus to last forever, is painful and repulsive. [Yes, thus to last one hour.] . . . The natural idea we have of a disembodied spirit is that of a wandering, restless ghost. [Yet, some people's notions leave our loved ones to wander thus through interminable ages.] As naturally as we breathe we seize upon the idea of a home for and an embodiment of the soul—one that is perfect and under complete control. [That is just what Paul says we *have*, as soon as the earthly home is dissolved. Just what John says we shall be, embodied personalities. Just as Jesus *is*, for we shall be like him.] Such a condition during our future existence can alone satisfy our desires. ***Any other condition would never have been dreamed of, but for enmity to the truth, and a false interpretation of the Scriptures.*** [The italics are ours, and we add, emphatically, AMEN!] . . . Human nature, to be complete, must have some kind of organism. [Angels have organisms, and we are to be as they are.] . . . Upon high and strictly rational grounds, we may assert that a bodily organism in the future life is a positive necessity of our nature. It is a revelation, not from the Bible alone, but from every human soul. [How cruel, then, to teach that for thousands, and probably tens of thousands of years, the soul shall be a disembodied spirit, "a restless, wandering ghost?" One hour of such nakedness would be as death itself. Let us believe the Bible, and not the terrible Roman dogma of an intermediate state.] . . . Dreamy and shadowy phantoms find no place in the Scriptures. The organisms of the dead are as real as those of angels. Let us have done with spiritualistic and Anti-Christian notions which reduce the universe to gas, and our deceased friends to atmospheric phenomena. We are not to become ghosts and nothings. . . . When we die we shall see friends and know them, as certainly before as after the resurrection. . . . When the eyes of mortals are closing in death, do they not frequently seem to open upon sweet and well-known faces? Do not dear and familiar names sometimes break from their closing lips? The welcome of friends long since dead is heard in the heavenly world before the farewells are hushed in this. There are moments when the physical organisms of this world are seen in company with the spiritual organisms of the other world, and where the blending voices of both worlds are audible."

It is sad to see one basking in such pure and comforting Bible and experimental truths, and then to see him drawn back, evidently reluctantly, by that relentless tether, to the chilling dogma of something, he knows not what, but which, in deference to the creed from which he dare not break away, he calls the resurrection. He flounders, and apologizes for this in the following unsatisfactory manner: "But if this spiritual organism be so complete, why the need of new resurrection bodies? What if we do not know? God says we are to have them, and this is enough." [The very thing which God does not say. The very thing of which Christ sought to disabuse the minds of the Sadducees, if you mean bodies to be taken on, ages hence.]

One would hardly suppose that, having so effectively disposed of the material body, sending it in his theology, where it is sent in philosophy, "into the vegetable and animal kingdom, into the atmosphere, and the clouds that float above us," we would ever find him poetizing among the tombs. But that tether, that dreadful tether, brings him down at last from the pure atmosphere of the Bible truth, and we find him burning up the world with the usual ceremony, and providing for the disembodied ghosts a luxury which he thus describes: "Would it not be a pleasant experience, as well as a dictate of philosophy, if in the graveyard of ourselves and friends, our spirits should at last meet to bid an eternal and ever-present welcome to each other, and a final farewell to the crumbling world and crumbling body?" [Why in a graveyard any more than elsewhere, seeing the bodies there have been dissipated "in the atmosphere and in the clouds?"]

To this we add the following from Dr. Curry, of the *Christian Advocate*, New York, who will hardly be denominated an iconoclast or a heretic or an infidel: "We are free to say that some things that we have heard and read about raising to immortality the material body—the breaking up of graves and the upsetting of tombstones at the 'resurrection'—may be questioned without incurring the guilt of heresy, and that the materialistic renderings of the language of our Lord and of St. Paul may, without offense, be re-examined. We certainly should feel free to do it."—*Christian Advocate*, Jan. 15, 1874.

Bishop Butler's famous *Analogy of Religion*, which has remained unanswered for 150 years because it is unanswerable, and which is a text book in every theological school in England and America, is based upon the doctrine that the body is no part of the man. In his

By far the most plausible as well as the most common argument in favor of a bodily resurrection is that which assumes that the resurrection is the bringing up of something which had gone under—something which had gone down. Dr. Edwards states the argument thus: "The resurrection is the resurging from death of that which died." Others ask, "What body is it that is sown?" and answer, "Clearly our bodies of flesh and blood," and add, "The soul does not die; it is the body that dies, and it is therefore the body which must be raised."

This whole argument is baseless, because founded upon an unscriptural as well as an unphilosophical idea of death. The body no more dies in the article of death than the soul dies then. It no more dies after what is called death than it died before. What men call death is simply

---

argument on the Future State, he says: "All presumption of death's being the destruction of living beings must go upon the supposition that they are compounded. . . . Now upon supposition that the living agent that each man calls himself is a single being, it follows that our organized bodies are no more ourselves or part of ourselves than any other matter around us. . . . It is as easy to conceive that we may exist out of bodies as in them. . . . Things of this kind unavoidably teach us to distinguish between these living agents, ourselves, and large quantities of matter in which we are very nearly interested. . . . After all, the relation a person bears to these parts of his body amounts to but this, that the living agent and those parts of the body mutually affect each other. . . . Our organs of sense and our limbs are certainly instruments which the living person, ourselves, makes use of to perceive and move with. There is not any probability that they are any more, nor consequently that we have any other kind of relation to them than what we have to any other foreign matter, formed into instruments of perception or motion, suppose into a microscope or staff. . . . And we have no reason to think we stand in any other kind of relation to any thing which we find dissolved by death."

Page after page of the Analogy is in this strain. It is the basis of the entire book. Whatever of value is found in the book is as dependent upon this assumption as are all the subsequent propositions of Euclid upon the propositions contained in his first book.

that event—that point of time—at which the vital forces cease to retain, in organized form, the earthy matter which composes the body. Every breath we exhale, every action of healthy vitality which throws off effete matter from any part of the body, is death as to that particle of matter which has thus fulfilled its mission in that body, and has gone hence by vital action itself to become dust again, and to be taken up, in due time, in other organisms, vegetable or animal, to thus live and die eternally by the laws which God has given, if being organized is life, and being disorganized is death; yet it is only inert matter in all these changes. In many instances this process of disorganization goes on rapidly for months, or even years, until that frame—that form—that body which was once glorious in its symmetry and strength becomes a mere feeble, decrepit mass of loathsome putrescence, with not one element of loveliness; and at last the vital spark ceases to preserve it any longer from absolute disintegration. Does that body die any more in this final escape of the vital force than when the other particles of it had died as to that body in escaping in advance, from a union with vitality? The body die, indeed! Solomon was wiser than ten thousand such philosophers when he said that in what men call death, "Dust returns to dust as it was, and the spirit returns to God who gave it." (Ec. xii., 7.)

Death is nothing more, nothing less, than this. It is a separation of the soul—the real man—from the dust of the earth, which was at the moment of separation in organized form. The spirit—the real man—goes to God its Father; the dust, to its kindred dust. Death is as predicable of the soul as of the body, for one separates from the other, each to seek its nearest of kin. The *man* dies—that union of inert matter with the spirit, which in common language we call man, dies,—the union ceases and the organism ceases; but neither the spirit nor the matter dies. Each exists afterwards in its appropriate sphere, though never to be reunited again in the same or a like organism. Dust to dust—the spirit with God.

CHAPTER XVI.

The Probable Nature of our Future Life.

WHETHER our immortality is attained by this process or that, both reason and revelation assure us that it will be purely spiritual and of eternal duration. But what may be an existence purely spiritual in its character, it is not probable that the utmost stretch of our imaginations ever conceived. Certainly, words cannot convey an idea of the properties of spirit, further than we have been made conversant with those properties in our own experiences. The language of earth refers only to things material and earthly, and is probably as inappropriate to the things of the spirit-life as the words which describe the properties of matter, which are realized only by sight, are to the man who never saw.

If in this world there are progressive developments of spirit-life, each successive stage opening a new plane with its new emotions, what shall we say of the probable character of spirit-life in the other world, when at once, or in rapid succession, there shall burst upon the spirit the realities of a sphere now unknown to it? That young mother, to-day for the first time looking upon the form of her first-born, is experiencing a soul-emotion to which she has hitherto been a stranger. Her love for that child is unlike, in character and degree, any love she has ever known before. It is a spirit-development, the springing into life of latent soul-capabilities, which may possibly be only one of a thousand such instances of spirit-growth which the ever new realities of the spirit-land may inspire. If no words or signs could ever open that sealed fountain until it was opened by the object on which a mother's love could rest, although she knew what was love for husband, and parents, and brothers, who need attempt to delineate the characteristics of the world of spirits by words applicable only to earth?

No doubt very much of the confusion which exists in the minds of people on this subject is the result of attempts to apply literally the extravagant poetic conceptions of immortality which are found in the Bible. Speaking of heaven, John calls it a new Jerusalem, and describes it as a walled city of no very extensive dimensions, but brilliant and costly in its appointments; yet certainly it would be too much of a prison house for spirits, if our conceptions of the capabilities of spirits are half-way correct. Other poets, probably quite as capable of doing the subject justice, have invested Paradise with the beauties of spring in the rural districts; making heaven an extensive plain, eternally bright, and perpetually brilliant with flowers, and abounding in choice fruits and cooling streams of pure water, not always omitting literal wine.

With all this, and much more like it, the heaven of not a few is to be pre-eminently a place of rest. They have dragged themselves, or have been driven, through a life of incessant toil, and nothing seems so heavenly as a place where there is nothing to do. Rest from trouble, rest from care, rest from toil, constitute their *beau idéal* of bliss, so much so that if it be suggested that probably spirits are ever active, they shake their heads with disapprobation.

A class of Christians, whose mental and moral make-up finds the perfection of earthly enjoyment in the excitement of a fervent type of religious exercises, think that the most desirable characteristics of the happy land will be its endless Sabbaths, and perpetual congregations of worshipers, where there will be loud singing and zealous shouting, not marred by the tones of any huge organ in the gallery.

To the heart that has been often broken by the removal hence from the family circle of the objects of its love, the chief charm of heaven will be its family reunions, with a hope that, being no death there, there will be no more parting.

Thus on, from the Indian, who thinks,

> "Admitted to that equal sky,
> His faithful dog will bear him company,"

through every grade of intellect and cultivation, we find diverse opinions of the probable details of the character and occupations of heaven, observing, as a general rule, that that becomes most prominent which is most longed for in this life.

The country rustic seizes most readily upon John's gorgeous city, with its foundation of jasper, and sardonyx, and sapphire, and gates of pearl, and its streets of gold. That is the perfection of splendor, in his estimation, and he thinks that city life, amidst such surroundings, would be most desirable.

On the other hand, the dweller in the city, whose vision is bounded by bleak walls and cheerless pavements, who never sees a green branch, or hears the notes of a happy bird, longs for a heaven of rural beauties and delights. He would never exchange Watts for John. Let his heaven be one of sweet fields beyond the swelling flood, all dressed in living green, where there are rocks, and hills, and brooks, and vales, with milk that is not diluted, and honey that is fresh from the comb. The little child, who was captivated by the splendor of a steamboat cabin, as contrasted with her own home, only played the grown up Christian, of average opinion and hopes, when she asked if heaven would be any prettier than that.

Many of our songs contribute, no doubt, to very erroneous views of the abode of immortals. It is, indeed, no longer taken to be an underground cavern, more thanks to science than to the popular interpretation of Scripture, however; but it is a "happy land, far, far, away." What right has any one to teach such a doctrine? Poets are unreliable theologians as a general thing. Heaven cannot be far away, whatever or wherever it may be. We know only this about it with certainty: There is no night there; no sickness, no crying, no hunger or thirst, no death; but the Redeemer and the redeemed are there, and the redeemed are like the Redeemer; each a pure spirit, yet each retaining such a personal identity that it shall be readily recognizable by fellow immortals.

There is a beauty in the conception that as the earth and other planets revolve around the sun as their center, so the sun, and other suns, the fixed stars, may revolve around still another center, and these larger centers still revolve around centers still larger, until at the inner center of all material existence, is found the throne of God. This is not only beautiful, but it is probable, as to the construction of the material universe, and not improbable as to God himself, who, as spirit, is omnipresent, yet is represented to our conceptions as having a seat of power and authority. These frequent representations cannot be all poetry. At least, it is not possible for us, in the body, to form a better idea of him than is afforded by such language as the Bible uses. But all this does not make our heaven "far, far away," or intimate that it is not a place or locality; it only makes it the more heavenly by conceiving that it is as large as the universe.

The chief difficulty in comprehending heaven grows out of our ignorance of the essence of spirit. After all, what is spirit? Man was created pure spirit, and as such, no doubt, had a separate existence before he entered the body which was formed for him of the dust of the ground. Is it unreasonable, therefore, to suppose that he shall have such an existence after leaving the body?

Perhaps the nearest approach that we can ever make to the substance of spirit is found in the capabilities of mind, which is spirit encased in an earthly body, the real immortal man itself. But mind is hardly local. It is here now, giving attention to weighing or measuring some material substance. In a moment it is yonder, among some ancient ruins, or surveying some modern enterprise. Now it goes away in quest of that great center where God is, and then returns to the sober duties of every-day life.

If mind, the man, encumbered by a fleshy body, can thus approximate omnipresence, what may we not attribute to the spirit-man when unclothed of this earthly house?

There is nothing in the Bible-account of the spirit-land that necessarily fixes it at a great distance from earth. When Saul called for Samuel he was not far away; and there are not wanting instances, well authenticated, of such spirit communings as indicate that if the departed do not hover around us as angels do, nay, become in some sense the guardian angels of those who are to become heirs of salvation, they may visit the earth without going beyond the bounds of their heavenly home.*

Dr. Whedon, one of the ripest scholars of the

---

* "There are seasons when the soul seems to recognize the presence of the departed, and to hold communion with them. They are like angelic visitants. We meet them in our lonely walks, in our deep and solemn meditations and in our closet communions. We meet them when the lengthening shadows hallow the even-tide. Mysterious and solemn is their communion. We meet them where sorrows encompass us round about, and hallowed is the influence their presence imparts. Who shall say that at such times there is not a real communion between the living and the dead? Who shall say that there is not then a real presence of the dead with the living? . . . There is a pernicious view in the religious world, by which the dead are disassociated from the living. It was the impression of Mr. Wesley, that the strong impressions on the mind of Swedenborg, of the presence of deceased friends at particular moments, was produced by their actual but invisible presence. Thousands of Christians have had, at times, as clear and overpowering a consciousness of the spiritual presence of departed friends as of their own self-being.

There is one other fact bearing on this subject which we cannot now forbear. It is the affecting recognition of the presence of the dead in Christ, which is sometimes realized by the dying saint. Parents have recognized departed children as present to welcome them, just at the moment of their own departure. So have children recognized the presence of a sainted father or mother. Also brothers and sisters have thus seemed to meet each other on the dividing line between this world and the next."—*Bishop Clark. Man All Immortal, page* 208, 209.

day, as well as one of the most profound metaphysicians, but withal a great stickler for a literal future resurrection (in a modified form, as we have seen), thus explains away the material portions of the body after it has been raised.

"While the material particles of the body are unchanged, the organism passes through a reorganizing and glorifying change. The same in material, it is new in arrangements, properties, and capabilities. It will be a spiritual body, and that body will be angel-like. By the body's becoming a spiritual body, we understand that it will become subtilized, so adjusted to the pure spirit, and so subjected in every part and particle to the volition and power of the spirit, that, while the spirit becomes, so to speak, more substantiated, the personal unit of the two natures possesses all the capabilities that our thoughts usually attribute to the pure spirit."

Very well; the body becomes pure spirit after all, only that in some way, "so to speak," it slightly *substantiates* that spirit, yet it is pure spirit in its attributes. One can hardly refrain from asking, why then all this pother about a resurrection of matter, which is only an insignificant part of the body after all, according to Dr. Whedon's theory, if in the end it becomes pure spirit? Is it because God can not furnish us a spiritual body without having a material body from which to make the spiritual? But since the immortal being, rebuilt by reuniting the long-separated soul and body, and by depriving the body of all its peculiar properties, except that it may yet "substantiate" the soul, has all the capabilities of pure spirit, there is not so much difference between materialists and spiritualists, except in the delay which the theory of the former causes. Whether this be a coming of Mahomet to the mountain, or the mountain to Mahomet, matters not.

There is, however, something so *spiritual* in the attributes of this spiritual body, as given by the Doctor, although, "so to speak, somewhat substantiated," that we adopt it as expressing views which are probably correct. "By volition it passes, with lightning rapidity, through nameless distances. It clairvoyantly sees, at volition, through a finite immensity."

That which follows is, if anything, better still, only we would attribute it to pure spirit, whether created in the image of God, as Adam was, and as man will be when divested of his form, or manufactured out of pre-existent matter, as Dr. Whedon supposes the spiritual body will be. It is entirely consistent with spirit demonstrations as recorded in the Bible, and no less authentic instances in more modern times:

"By volition it transforms itself into any shape, and invests itself with a countless variety of properties and phenomenal presentations. It can become as the dark rolling cloud, the flashing lightning, the solid rock. And yet it will have a normal figure and face, which will at once be the true expression of its essential nature, and will reveal to the intuition of fellow-celestials the particular personality, and perhaps the entire past history of the individual. When asked, Will the glorified bodies have teeth? we reply, If they please; and eat with them too, as the angels did who visited Abraham. If asked, Will they have hair? we reply, Yes, if they please, and shining raiment too, as the two angels did before the apostles at the ascension. Nothing is more clear, we think, than that varying phenomenal form and properties are more or less at the command both of the pure spirit and the union of spirit with spiritual body."*

Of these sentiments, so generally both philosophically and Scripturally correct, we add only that they seem to be the strugglings of an independent thinker to rise above the logical conclusions of his false premises and the errors and prejudices of early education. Both reason and revelation teach that the future man will be pure spirit, "as the angels of God in heaven." So says Dr. Whedon; yet, as though that were too much to attribute to the just made perfect, to *man all immortal*, he qualifies his otherwise happy conception by saying "the spirit becomes, so to speak, more substantiated."

It may be difficult to comprehend how man, whom we know now only in an earthly body, can exist pure spirit, "as the angels of God in heaven;" yet that is what Christ says of him, and we prefer such authority to any other.

Give us, then, this sublime conception of the perpetual continuance of life, terminating in a life which shall be "as the angels of God in heaven," without any hint that there must be some modification of so glorious an existence

* These attributes of spirit give great plausibility to the theory of the "appearances" of the Saviour after his resurrection, given in the chapter on the resurrection of Christ, and most satisfactorily account for the flesh and bones which he announced that he had. The Bible is full of facts which authorize the views here so ably set forth, and so, also, do well authenticated instances of spirit manifestations of a later day, whether the immediate agent were called a witch or a medium. It is no longer considered a mark of profound wisdom to dismiss cases of clairvoyance or spiritual manifestations with a sneer, as was once the method; and, although there is a world of fraud and imposture in what is called modern spiritualism, the man writes himself a dunce who assumes to treat it all as beneath his notice, or pronounce it all a delusion and imposition.

by a union, at some future time, with something of an earthly, material nature, which will thereafter make us more like earth. Our departed friends are certainly pure spirits now, and they are certainly in heaven, even by the concessions of those who believe in literal material resurrection. (See extract from Bishop Clark, elsewhere.) They are with Christ, and they are like Christ. They are *now*, as Christ *is*. Well might David say: "I shall be satisfied when I awake with thy likeness." Who can ask anything more? And why should good men labor to teach that the heavenly life shall ever be anything less?

We close this chapter with a few suggestions which some may consider speculative. They may be true or false, without affecting the general doctrine of the book.

Shall we recognize friends in the spirit life? Certainly. Why not? Being "the children of the resurrection," and "as the angels of God in heaven," the bonds which shall unite us may not be so selfish and exclusive as are the ties of kindred and the bonds of friendships here, but there will be, no doubt, a renewal and a recognition of the loves and friendships of this life in the life beyond. There are too many instances of spirit communings, not to speak of spirit manifestations, here, to doubt the interest of the departed in those left behind, and, of course, in those of like relationship in the land of spirits. That vague notion which too many entertain of spirits, that they are clouds or atmosphere or undefined shapes, has no countenance in the Bible or in common sense or in experience. The spirit form, the spirit body, will be well defined, and will certainly be recognizable in the heavenly home, as it often is by clairvoyance here, and by the dying, while they may yet communicate with those around.

Will children remain children in the spirit-life? We cannot tell, but we hope they will. There is a world of beauty in the language of Christ: "Of such is the kingdom of heaven." There is an instinctive love for childhood which never dies in the pure and the good, and which is not dependent upon any relationship to the child itself. The cynic who is not moved by the loveliness of childhood is a monomaniac, and by that much, at least, unfitted for good society, whether that deplorable state has been reached by vice, or crime, or selfishness. If the presence of children is so desirable in the social circle, even in the steamboat, or rail-car, or stage-coach, who does not hope that children will remain children in the land of spirits? Let them increase in knowledge eternally, but let their "spiritual body," their "mansion," their "house not made with hands," forever remain infantile, as we knew them in the earth-life.

Will idiots and imbeciles remain feeble-minded in heaven? We suppose not. Science has often demonstrated that, in many cases, idiocy is the result of physical malformation. Why may not all cases of mental weakness be, though it be congenital and possibly hereditary? The intellectual giants of earth may not tower above others in the land of spirits. Certainly an intellect of any type which has been devoted here to selfish and wicked purposes will not share in the bliss which we are taught by reason and revelation to expect for those who seek to do the will of God on earth.

Men often speak derisively of those whom they choose to regard as not very intellectual, and say "they know just enough to be religious." Perhaps among the greatest surprises which await us in the land of immortals will be one not greatly unlike that experienced by the rich man of whom Christ speaks. He had been a sharp trader and a success in life, as men measure success. He was probably benevolent and kind, else Lazarus would not have called upon him habitually for alms. Yet in all his life he had done nothing which could be available in securing happiness in the life beyond, while Lazarus, contemned as a beggar by the busy, happy, healthy crowd, had been cultivating that heavenly-mindedness which eminently fitted him for the society of the good in that spirit-land. Thus many who have contemned the religious obscurity of others as contrasted with their own mental or social position, may be surprised to find that, after all, these were wiser in life than those who had despised them. Hence it is not improbable that those whom we pity, and denominate imbeciles, may at once take higher rank in the land of immortals than some who have occupied the highest social and intellectual positions. It was for misusing his one talent, not because he had but one, that the unfaithful servant was condemned—it was for improving what they had, not because they had two, or five, or ten talents, that the faithful stewards were rewarded.

CHAPTER XVII.

The Condition of the Wicked.

IN the preceding chapters we have spoken of the mode of human immortality in general, referring for illustration chiefly to the condition of the righteous. It must not be inferred from this that we would teach that either the Bible or reason warrants the assumption, that in the life to come there will be no difference between those who served God on earth and those who served him not. On the contrary, both reason and revelation teach that there will be a vast and changeless difference.

While, therefore, the sacred writers seem to have struggled to find modes of speech and illustrations from the most joyous and delightful things of life to impress us with the desirableness of the life beyond, for those who, by patient continuance in well doing, seek for glory, it has equally had recourse to the most terrible things by which to convey an idea of the misery of those who reject the Saviour, and remain disobedient to the commands of God.

Of the wicked it is said, They shall go away into everlasting punishment. Their anguish is described as the burning of a fire that is not quenched, as the gnawings of a worm that never dies, as abiding in outer darkness, where there are weeping and wailing and the gnashing of teeth, and, more fearful than all, as being punished with everlasting destruction from the presence of the Lord, and from the glory of his power. It can, therefore, be no matter of trifling import to die under condemnation.

In a ruder and more sensuous age, and even yet among those who are incapable of appreciating the greater pains of mental agony, these terrible figures of speech were received as veritable realities, and in imagination the infernal regions of Pluto were accepted as the gospel abodes of the lost, with a personal devil, and legions of fiends and furies, and literal fire and endless smoke. Thitherward the souls of the wicked were sent at death, and, after the resurrection and judgment, soul and body were to be locked forever in a vast prison, burning eternally with fire and brimstone.

The Bible gives no authority for such a disposition of the wicked. Its fearful descriptions of the anguish of those who have been disobedient, when properly interpreted by the Bible itself, are even more dreadful than any physical sufferings, but they do not authorize the hell of the middle ages, or of the less cultivated and more brutal of this age.

Neither are the wicked to be annihilated. The immortal man is still in the image of God, though fallen; and, though under condemnation for sin, and unfitted for the society of the good, he lives, simple spirit, after having laid aside his house of clay at the close of his earthly probation.

There is nothing inconsistent with analogy or the Bible in supposing that, so far as locality is concerned, the good and the bad live together hereafter as here. There are good angels and bad angels spoken of in the Bible, yet they are not separated by distance, wide and impassable as the moral gulf may be between them.

The parables which speak of separating the tares from the wheat and the sheep from the goats can not be made to do service in proving distinct and distant places of abode for the good and the bad, unless we put the parables "on all fours," and prove also a literal throne, with a literal king upon it, always facing towards the same point of heaven's compass, with the right hand always turned towards the righteous and the left hand always towards the wicked. To our mind such expressions as "come, ye blessed," "depart, ye cursed," have no reference to locality. Those who so interpret them may do so without doing any violence to the lesson to be enforced by Christ, while we see in them even a more terrible retribution than such a material separation implies. Such a literalizing of the language of Christ will require a belief that the righteous are to *sit* for ever, for they are to "*sit down* with Abraham and Isaac and Jacob in the kingdom."

In the account which Christ gives of the rich man and Lazarus, the two were within seeing and hearing distance. The great gulf between them was the unalterableness of their moral characters; that of Lazarus being a passport to fellowship with the good, but that of the rich man keeping him a great way off. One was comforted in realizing the fruition of his faith in the midst of sufferings, while the other was tormented in being not only deprived of his earthly joys, but in having no fellowship with the pure and holy of the land of spirits.

Even if the theory of some be true, that from the beginning of the life of immortality all shall tend upward in moral and intellectual character, the good and the bad alike, there will yet be an impassable gulf between them. The want of moral fitness for the society of Abraham was a gulf which could never be crossed by the departed rich man. In this life the wicked usually wax worse and worse, deceiving and being deceived, until their last moments; while the path of the just grows brighter and brighter. If there is anything in the article of death or in the after-life which may check the momentum of earthly habits in either direction, it has never been revealed by observation or by revelation. But assuming that it may be, and that from the hour the man leaves the body in which he has never sought to please God or love him, he begins to lead a better life, yet he must see those who were wiser and better during their probation forever nearer to God than he himself can be. This gulf is impassable.

We can hardly conceive of a more marked difference of character than that of Samuel and that of Saul; yet, when Samuel foretold the death of Saul and his sons, it was by announcing that to-morrow they would be with him. If heaven were a separate place, far removed from the locality of hell, this would be impossible. Samuel and Saul were together in the land of immortals, yet they were as unlike in moral character and in personal happiness as they had been on earth. The gulf which separated them was no wider now than then, and they were no more companions in the spirit-land than they had been on earth. The wretchedness of Saul was not alleviated by the death of his body, for his anguish was soul-anguish.

Why may not the good and the bad live

together in the spirit-land as they do here, and as good and bad angels do there? The wicked shall there have no power to trouble, and, doubtless, the distinction will be more marked, more perceptible, than here. No robe of mock righteousness will shield the hypocrite, and no garment of outward morality will conceal the inward hatred of the heart, with its fountains of corruption ever flowing. This of itself will be an undying torment, a fire which nothing can quench.

What burning could be so terrible as a conscious existence among the pure and the holy, yet morally so far from them that approach and association were impossible? Everlasting destruction from the presence or favor of the Lord, and from the glory of his power, is the most terrible picture of the reward of the wicked. The recollection of opportunities slighted, and of misspent time, will be a perpetual remorse, more painful to the immortal man than the gnawings of any worm upon the body; and what darkness could be so unendurable as to be shut out from the favor and glory of the Lord? Those who insist on a literal place of burnings little appreciate the sinfulness of sin, and underrate the extent of the punishment of those who, knowing their duty during their probationary period, did it not.

The flames which tormented the rich man in hell were not from without, but from within. He was not in a literal lake of fire and brimstone, but fire more consuming by far was within him. Like the rich fool, who had fed his soul on much goods, by ministering only to the lusts of the flesh and the desires of the eye, whose god was his belly, and who minded only earthly things, he now found that the real man, dispossessed of these sources of happiness, had nothing on which the spirit could subsist. The distinctions which wealth had given were all gone, and in that land where moral character alone was the measure of worth, he saw the man whom he had contemned as a beggar now in the society of Abraham and the good of all previous ages, while his only associates were such as had been vile, and low, and sensual on earth like himself though clothed in purple and fine linen, still vile, and low, and sensual in the land of immortality. Could any flames from without so torment? Could any worm within a material body so gnaw as that consciousness of a misspent life would forever disturb a soul, lost? How significant the language of Christ: "What will it profit a man if he gain the whole world and lose his own soul? or what would a man give in exchange for his soul?"

Living in sight of the throne, yet not daring to approach it; feeling the power of the Lord, but partaking of none of the glory of that power; seeing Abraham, and Isaac, and Jacob, and thousands of personal acquaintances, whose humble lives of devotion to God were the butt of ridicule on earth, now clothed in the righteousness of faith, and living with the Lord, and being like him, while they, unclothed of their earthly treasure, have their moral rottenness all exposed—what torment! What an endless burning!

CHAPTER XVIII.

A few Words about Inspiration, Hell, Heaven, General Resurrection and the Day of Judgment.

LET it not be said that in this book we deny the inspiration of the Scriptures. Nothing could be further from the truth. If the reader *infers* from the views we have taken that this is so, let him state that such is his *inference*, not that it is our declaration. If he constructs a syllogism and reaches this conclusion, let him state it as a *conclusion*, not as a truth. His premises may be very faulty, and his conclusions may likewise be faulty; but above all let him be charitable, for the papist proves the same thing of him by the same process; feet-washing Baptists prove the same thing in the same way, and so on through the whole line of theological differences of opinion. It is the cheapest argument in the world, and, therefore, the most readily resorted to by the feeble-minded. No others use it, except where the thing is openly avowed. In our views of inspiration we are in good company. That standard theological work of this generation, McClintock and Strong's *Encyclopedia*, says: "Plenary inspiration is a phrase nowhere warranted by the Scriptures as predicated of themselves."

Let no one say that we deny that there is a hell. We do nothing of the kind. We believe and teach, as the Bible does, that there is a hell, whose burnings are eternal, but we do not believe that it is located in *Gehenna*, in the valley of the Sons of Hinnom; neither do we believe or teach that there is, or ever was, or ever will be, any part of the universe of God which is a lake of fire and brimstone, from which the smoke of torment ascends forever and ever. If the reader *infers* from this that we believe there is no hell, let him be honest and truthful, for whoso loveth and maketh a lie—whoso misrepresents his brother—shall have his portion in the lake of fire and brimstone, whatever that is; and we are free to confess that theological disputants are not always candid in stating the views of others—let him be truthful and say that he *infers* from our views that we teach that there is no hell, and not say that we teach anything of the kind.

Let no one say that we teach that there is no such place as Heaven because we do not believe that some special portion of God's creation is walled in with jasper, garnished with all manner of precious stones, and built within with pure gold, like unto glass, as the prison-house of the immortal, God-like man. The heaven of the Bible and of reason is so much grander than that, that we teach of a better country. But if any one *infers* that heaven is not a place if it is not a large city of indescribable splendor such as John saw, let him frankly state the case as his *inference*, not as our teaching. If he constructs a syllogism from his own fancy, and reaches this conclusion let him be honest—honesty is the best policy, even in theology—and let him say that such is his conclusion from his premises, not the teachings of this book.

Let no one say that we deny the resurrection of the dead. We do nothing of the kind. If the New Testament does not teach the resurrection of the dead, it teaches nothing. If any one *infers*, from the fact that we deny the resurrection of the material body, that, therefore, we deny the resurrection of the dead, let him state this as his *inference*, not as our teaching. If he cannot conceive how there can be an immortality without a body made of clay, let him say so; but let him not say that we teach no resurrection. The book is pre-eminently a book teaching the resurrection of the dead after the pattern shown to the disciples on the Mount of Transfiguration, and after the teachings of Christ, though not after the traditions of men.

Let no one say that we deny the doctrine of a general judgment, because we believe that the departed man goes at once to his place with an unchangeable character, and that there will be no such an event as a "resurrection morning" and a "judgment day," such as is often taught from the pulpits of the land. All of the moral sanctions of the Bible, particularly of the New Testament, find their authority in the great revealed truth which announces that "God hath appointed a day in which he will judge the world in righteousness by that man whom he hath ordained." Like all other essential Bible truths this is abundantly corroborated by the judgment and reason of man, and even if we found much less authority for it in the Bible we should be slow to shake public confidence in it, seeing that without such a doctrine the restraints against vice would be so enfeebled as to return Christendom to a worse than savage lawlessness.

We trust that we may be pardoned for devoting here a few paragraphs to this subject in elucidation of the Bible teachings, as we read and understand the Bible.

Peter says, (2 Pet., iii., 7): "The heavens and the earth, which are now, are kept in store, reserved unto fire against the day of judgment." This is, we believe, the most direct passage from which the idea of a "day of judgment" is deducible. We have shown in our chapter on the second coming of Christ that this referred to some event which the Christians of that time were "looking for and hasting unto." Whatever it was must have been nigh to them, and so it was, and so it came in less than six years from the time of the writing.

Perhaps we may find some clue to the utter destructiveness of this fire which shall dissolve the heavens, and melt the elements (v. 12), by referring to the fact that Peter also says: "The heavens that were of old, and the earth, and the world that then was, *perished*" by being overflowed with water, (Greek, *apolluo*—were destroyed). Peter means nothing more than this, in reference to the on-coming calamity. How utterly the world *perished*, or was *destroyed* by the flood, we well know. We do not see how any man can claim Peter for authority for any other kind of a destruction of the present heaven and earth than the destruction caused by that flood, in the light of Peter's own explanation by his reference to the local flood which is described by Moses. Let him who can believe such, so believe; we cannot. It is a method of interpretation at war with every law of exegesis.

But, says the objector, does not Peter look for "new heavens and a new earth"? Most certainly, "according to His promise." That we may know what this is, let us look at the "promise." "Behold I create new heavens and a new earth," (Is. lxv., 17). This is the promise. Then what follows? Men shall build houses, sinners shall live to be a hundred years old, the elect shall live to be as old as a tree, the lion shall eat straw like the bullock, and the serpent shall feed on dust, and much more of that kind. Is this anything like the heaven which men usually locate on the new earth which is to come out of the fire after the dissolution and meltings of the judgment day? If the things which belong to that new heaven are figurative, why should the burning, and melting, and dissolution all be literal? If the elect are to die even when they reach the age of a tree, there will be death in the new heavens and the new earth; and even if sinners are to be accused at the age of a hundred years, then there are to be sinners there. We most affectionately beg our readers to "re-examine and re-state" their views on this subject. It will bear further investigation.

But Peter says: "The day of the Lord will come, etc." We have referred to this in another chapter, and add in this connection only this: Isaiah (xiii., 13) calls the day of the destruction of Babylon the "day of the Lord," "the day of his fierce anger," which shall shake the heavens and the earth. A similar hyperbole is found in Isaiah 24th, in which "the earth is utterly broken down and clean dissolved." (v. xix.) Yet we never heard this chapter quoted as authority for a day of judgment or the burning up of the world.

Why not accept the plain, simple, and reasonable teachings of Christ on this subject? Why should they be distorted to prove so absurd and unscriptural a proposition as that which is contained in the notion of a "general judgment" after a "general resurrection," in which all who shall have lived on earth are to be brought before a literal throne, with literal books to be opened, and literal angels to act as bailiffs, and a literal traversing of every act and every thought of lives which had ended millions of years before, most of them in utter obscurity? And all this is to be done in one day—literally within one twenty-four hours; and indeed in only a very small part of that day, for the dead in Christ have to be raised first, then those who are alive have to be changed, and then the judgment, all on the same day. To extend the time beyond one literal day of twenty-four hours is to abandon this entire theory of the resurrection and the judgment. If it may lap over into another day it may into two days, into ten days, into ten years, into thousands, into millions of years, and this would destroy the whole theory and bring it in harmony with the doctrine of Christ on this subject—the doctrine of reason and experience.

We cannot speak certainly, but we do not believe that any man, of any age, in any time, of any degree of cultivation, was ever satisfied with his own reasonings and the reasonings of the books on this subject which ended in the calling of the happy from heaven and the damned from hell for a few hours that they might reinhabit their old bodies, and, a second time, hear their doom and depart to the right or left according to their character. To say that it must be postponed until the Almighty finds out how much evil a bad man has done, following the stream of his influences to the end, and how much good an upright man has done, following the stream of good influences in the same way to its end, sounded to us like blasphemy when we heard it with emphasis in childhood—it sounds no better now. We do not say that this is blasphemy in the mouths of those who use it, but it would be in our mouth. "Known unto God are all his works from the beginning of the world." We have referred to the teachings of Christ on this subject. Any word of Christ, half so directly teaching a resurrection of the body, would be seized upon as unanswerable; why is not this: "*Now* is the judgment of this world"? (John ii., 31.) And again: "The Father *judgeth* no man, but *hath committed* all judgment to the Son," (John v. 22), and "*Hath given* him authority to execute judgment." (v. 27.) Whatever. is meant by this judgment is *now* taking place. So manifestly does this refer to a final judgment that Dr. Whedon in his notes says: "Be it specially noted that during this passage the entire future of death and resurrection is held as conceptually present." We would substitute *actually* for *conceptually*, and heartily agree with the commentator. On John v., 27, he says: "We have in the present passage a brief but most explicit description of the simultaneous resurrection and universal judgment of mankind." This, too, we most cordially endorse, except that by the context the Doctor refers it to' the far-off future resurrection of the body. We assume and we think we have shown that the resurrection—the *anastasis*—follows immediately upon death, and the judgment is simultaneous therewith, as every Christian but soul-sleepers practically admits, in conceding that the soul goes at once to a place of conscious joy or misery, which it could not do intelligently, except that the judge had exercised judgment in the case, for from the decision of that hour there is no appeal. The "final judgment," as taught in some pulpits, is not for a re-hearing of the case, but only for an intensifying of a judgment already passed. We have already shown that by authority of Peter "The great and terrible day of the Lord, spoken of by Joel," (Acts ii., 17,) referred to the times in which Peter lived, a part of which was fulfilled in the day of Pentecost, and a part in the terrible visitation so graphically predicted by Peter in his second epistle, third chapter.

There are, then, a general resurrection and a general judgment. The dead live again, and the good are rewarded and the bad are punished; but instead of limiting all this to the few hours which are usually supposed to embrace them, or instead of beginning them at some far-off future, and extending them indefinitely or eternally thence forward (for if extended beyond the twenty-four hours they may be extended eternally—if the word day is not limited to twenty-four hours of our time, and means only a period, it may as well have begun with Adam as to begin millions of years hence and extend thence forward indefinitely), we begin them where Christ began them. Abraham lived with God, and had been judged; Lazarus lived with Abraham, and had been judged; the rich man was in torment, having been judged. "*Now is the judgment of this world,*" says Christ, and we believe his words in preference to any creed made by man.

CHAPTER XIX.

CONCLUDING REMARKS.

WE conclude with the chapter which probably some would have placed in the beginning. We have often been met, during the years that we have been preaching the doctrine of the resurrection of the dead and its kindred topics as herein set forth, by appeals not to disturb the settled faith of the people; as though it were almost a sin to jostle men out of the ruts of thought and opinion along which they and their fathers had so long driven unmolested. In one sense it is mischievous. It is such an affliction for some men to think, that it is almost cruel to disturb their drowsiness, and this is not applicable to the pew only, for some men who occupy the pulpit find it so much easier to accept Milton, and Pollock, and Young, as their teachers, than to inquire in the Bible whether these things are so, that they preach from year to year without any farther investigation than the "standard authors" afford. The suggestion partakes of insufferable cowardice.

On the subject discussed in these pages, we have found that many pastors not only entertain doubts on the subject of a bodily resurrection at the so-called end of the world, but they entertain decided convictions that the doctrine is not authorized by the Bible and is opposed by well established philosophy; yet, for prudential reasons, they continue to preach the dogma according to the creed, or they say nothing on the subject at all, because it is so much easier to jog along, receiving their stipend from a satisfied flock than it is to arouse thought on any subject. Neither can it be denied that the ecclesiastical lash has had something to do in this enforced silence. Until within a short time every ecclesiastical organization built its iron bedstead which was to be the exact measure of fraternity. Happily, however, that day is past forever in the Christian Church, and nothing but a denial of the most fundamental articles of faith is any longer a bar to Christian fellowship.*

That the pulpit has lost much of its power over the pew is undeniable. To a certain extent this is legitimate and desirable. The peripatetic school master was once an oracle of wisdom in the neighborhood, for he alone of all the adults could read, write and cipher; but he is not so now, and never will be again, because an educated community is his equal in learning, and he now commands only the respect due his honorable calling, while he fills that calling honorably.

The pre-eminence of the pulpit over the pew in point of learning, to say nothing of a kind of superstitious reverence for the place, once gave it a factitious authority which, happily, it can never have again, while an educated laity rivals it in Bible research, and in labors of love and self-consecration to the cause of truth.

---

* As this page is in the hands of the printer, the Chicago Presbytery has vindicated the truth of this proposition by sustaining, by a large majority, the talented Dr. David Swing, though he has confessedly departed from the old formulas of the Presbyterian creed. The result of that trial is indicative of the larger liberality of modern Christianity.

The spiritual wants of men, when properly aroused, will take them to the congregation of worshipers that they may obtain that spiritual food which can be had nowhere else as it can in the sanctuary, in the communion of kindred spirits; but this is often at a great sacrifice, when their intelligent convictions are outraged by being compelled to listen to a homily on the resurrection of the material body which does violence to the teachings of the Bible and to common sense, delivered by some one who has not ingenuity enough to eliminate nineteen-twentieths of the matter before undertaking the task, as is now the custom in educated circles, as we have seen by quotations from men of learning and position.

We would not have the pulpit turned into a platform for scientific lectures. Its one theme should be repentance toward God and faith in the Lord Jesus Christ. There is no refinement in modern society which demands any modification of the style of Paul and Peter when they preached Jesus and the resurrection as the hope of man, but when, instead of this, the soul which is hungering for spiritual food is treated to a discourse on the resurrection of the dead, which is substantially a repetition of Young's "Last Day," the thinking man retires in disappointment and disgust. The language may be somewhat different but the argument is all to the point of a literal resurrection of the material body however much that may have been scattered, and at the sound of Gabriel's trump they say:

"Now charnels rattle, scattered limbs and all
The various bones, obsequious to the call,
Self-moved, advance: the neck perhaps to meet
The distant head, the distant legs the feet.

Dreadful to view! See through the dusky sky
Fragments of bodies in confusion fly,
To distant regions journeying, there to claim
Deserted members and complete the frame."

Is it any wonder that many thinking men have been repelled by such senseless jargon, and have been led to doubt human immortality altogether, or to embrace only the cheerless, Christless notions which are taught at spiritual *séances*, because they are both more Scriptural and reasonable than such absurdities?

It is our profound conviction that very few of the thinking men of the age believe in the doctrine of the resurrection of the dead, as taught in the dark ages, so graphically epitomized in the extract from Young just given. That there are such feeble, yet such learned efforts to reconcile it to the known laws of God, as we have seen, is evidence of this.*

But these modifiers of the "creed" are very much in the dilemma in which Mr. Beecher was recently placed by a question. Being asked if he believed in the doctrine of the decrees, as Calvin taught it, he answered: "I believe in the doctrine of the decrees as it is taught in the Bible, and as John Calvin would teach it if he were alive now, and knew what we know." Happy Mr. Beecher! A believer in Calvinism, as Calvinism would be with the light of this century shining upon the good Calvin!

We imagine that these modifiers of the doctrine as it was delivered to the saints a hundred

---

*"For a long time we have noticed a gradual departure from the clear and definite assertion of the fact and the mode of the resurrection of the body as we used to hear it in sermons or read it in theological treatises. This change has appeared in the reticence or the vagueness of utterance on the subject by the best class of thinkers." —*Dr. D. Curry in Christian Advocate.*

or five hundred years ago, if asked, Do you believe in the resurrection of the body? would answer: "Yes, as the discoveries of modern science have modified the doctrine; by eliminating all foreign matter and all useless appendages."

Believing, therefore, that the Christian church would be more aggressive at home and abroad, and that the consolations of a Christian faith would be greater in sickness and in health, and its triumphs more marked in death, if that gloomy view of the life beyond were wholly abandoned, and the faith of Paul and Stephen substituted in its stead, we send out this little book to do what it may toward the desirable end. It goes out with no flourish of trumpets, or pretensions to great learning, or with any ambitious expectations that it will suddenly revolutionize the sentiments of everybody. That it will do something in that direction we are sure. Its doctrines, often preached to large congregations, have been heard by the common people gladly, and many who have not had the boldness to declare their convictions in the pulpit have, at least, ceased to preach as they once did.

We may be pardoned for saying that the immediate occasion for embodying our views in this form was the more than ordinary Christian strength which such sentiments gave to the dying daughter, whose happy death is alluded to in Chapter thirteen, with a hope that the perusal of these pages may remove the dread of death and especially of the grave from many a timid, trusting one such as she was, as this faith did from her.

The sentiment of her dying experience was not an accident nor a recent revelation. It was the fixed and intelligent faith of her life, which had been one of peculiar affliction. Among the relics which we prize is her Bible, with the passages marked which gave her this belief; and a blank-book, with many fugitive pieces of poetry to the same purport. We copy the following anonymous scrap, not so much for its poetic merit, as for the tribute it bears to her taste and sentiment, and also, as conveying a doctrine worthy the Christian religion:

"There is no death! The stars go down
To rise upon some fairer shore,
And, bright in Heaven's jeweled crown,
They shine forever more.

"There is no death! The dust we tread
Shall change beneath the summer showers
To golden grain, or mellow fruit,
Or rainbow-tinted bowers.

"The granite rocks disorganize
To feed the hungry moss they bear,
The forest leaves drink daily life
From out the viewless air.

"There is no death! The leaves may fall
The flowers may fade and pass away,
They only wait through wintry gloom
The coming of the May.

"There is no death! The angel form
Walks o'er the earth with silent tread;
He bears our best loved friends away,
And then we call them "dead."

"He leaves our hearts all desolate,
He plucks our sweetest flowers,
Transferred to realms of bliss, they now
Adorn immortal bowers.

"The bird-like voice, whose joyous tones
Made glad this scene of sin and strife,
Sings now in everlasting song
Amid the tree of life.

"Born into that undying life,
They leave us but to come again,
With joy we welcome them—the same,
Except in sin and pain."

We close with an extract from a late sermon by Rev. Henry Ward Beecher. We are aware that he is not authority on any theological dogma among dogmatic theologians. Nothing is easier, or more common, than for profound (?) preachers to curl the lip and say, with wonderful significance: "Humph! That is just like Beecher!" But notwithstanding all that, the thinking minds of the country give very respectful attention to his opinions—indeed, as the Chicago *Evening Journal* said not long since, "by his genius, and without any direct effort, he has more influence upon the ministerial profession than all the theological seminaries combined." The following is the passage, taken from a sermon of 1873, entitled "The Ages to Come":

"Some believe that this mortal body rises again. Thank God, not I! I have had enough of it. And when once the earth takes it, the earth may keep it. The tree is welcome to what it can get of me. Says the apostle:

"'There is a natural body, and there is a spiritual body.' 'Flesh and blood cannot inherit the kingdom of God.'

"Good by, old flesh and blood! I am bound for God's kingdom without you.

"What it will be to be without them, I cannot tell; but I know it will be magnificent—never tiring any more, unwearied and unweariable, with nothing to hinder, and everything to help. However it may be in the present, 'in the ages to come,' over the mountains, across the valleys, behind the clouds, beyond all calculable periods, there will be a state in which we shall have dropped this natural body, and shall be endued with our spiritual body, whatever that is, and shall be free from the circumscription and weariness of this mortal condition. We shall be 'Sons of God.' Who can tell how he will seem, or how he will be, then? And who can conceive of that state in which every eye shall shine on him like a star; in which every heart shall impress itself on his heart, and make it better, and give it an impulse in the right direction, so that every being shall imprint on him some glorious aspect; so that every single creature of the whole realm, lifted into the highest state, shall bring balm and sweetness to every other one; when all hindrances shall be gone, and sorrowing and sighing shall have passed away, and singing shall have taken its place, and God shall wipe the tears from every eye—who can imagine that?

"It will transcend any image that you make of it. Draw from the heavens; draw from all that there is on earth; draw what you can through the channels of inspiration and of revelation; collect and cluster together the things which men have agreed to consider most admirable; and from these form pictorial parables of the City with its golden streets, with its gates of pearl, with its walls of precious stones, with its beautiful gardens, with its flowing rivers, and with its trees whose leaves are for the healing of the nations: picture as you may the future state, from oriental or monarchical conditions, or from the household and the commonwealth as they now exist; from any and all of these form your conception of it in any way that you please; but remember that when you have made it just as bright as your imagination can sketch it, when your fancy, architecturally, has wrought as skillfully as it can, and everything has been carried to the highest pitch that your earthly powers will allow, your conception will yet be imperfect. For the sweet apostle, looking upon you as a father upon his children, says,

"'It doth not yet appear what we shall be.'

"You have gathered from the cradle purity of idea, and clasp and cling of faith; you have gathered from rich companionship what is the thrill and the joy of the higher life; you have gathered from the patriarch and the matron—saints not yet gone home to glory—dignity and patience, and all that makes generosity and magnanimity; you have gathered your best fruits, and fashioned them into single characters, and into ranks, and into communities, and into nations; and you have combined all these things in your conception of the resplendent throne of the All-Father. But, saith the sweet apostle again,

"'It doth not yet appear.'

"Certainly not, brethren. And if you still add nation after nation, and age after age, to that conception, it will fall short of what the future is to reveal of the goodness of God through the Lord Jesus Christ."

www.ingramcontent.com/pod-product-compliance
Lightning Source LLC
LaVergne TN
LVHW012328100826
845148LV00017B/395

* 9 7 8 1 4 2 5 5 2 0 9 8 4 *